Understanding Children

Maggie Durran

Marshall Pickering

OTHER BOOKS BY MAGGIE DURRAN:

Dear God – most of the time you're quite nice
Dear God – if I ruled the world
Beginnings
Creation: enjoy and discover
Hello – I'm a person too
Children of the Troubles
Single parent – a personal story
The wind at the door

Marshall Morgan and Scott
Marshall Pickering
3 Beggarwood Lane, Basingstoke, Hants RG23 7LP, UK

Copyright © 1987 by Maggie Durran

First published in 1987 by Marshall Morgan and Scott Publications Ltd
Part of the Marshall Pickering Holdings Group
A subsidiary of the Zondervan Corporation

All rights reserved. No part of this publication may be reproduced, stored in a retrieval system, or transmitted, in any form or by any means, electronic, mechanical, photocopying, recording or otherwise, without the prior permission in writing, of the publisher

All Bible quotations taken from the New International Version, reprinted by permission of Hodder and Stoughton Ltd., and the International Bible Society

The chart on page 114 is reprinted by permission of The Open University.

British Library Cataloguing in Publication Data
Durran, Maggie
  Understanding children.
  1. Parenting—Religious aspects—
  Christianity
  I. Title
  261.8'35874   HQ755.8
  ISBN 5–551–01419–9
Text Set in 10 on 11 Times by
Input Typesetting Ltd, Wimbledon, London
Printed in Great Britain by Guernsey Press Ltd, Guernsey, C.I.

To my parents

With thanks to Steven Plummer for help in the final stages of this project. Thanks also to Christopher Ball, Matthew Ball and Richard Clarke for their illustrations.

CONTENTS

Introduction

1. **Esteem and respect** — 7
   Self-esteem and self-respect – messages
   Mutual awareness and respect
     Responsibility

2. **Spiritual development and the church** — 25
   Spiritual growth
   Family prayers
   Church and family

3. **A child's view of life** — 34
   Power of parents
   Religious beliefs
   Questions

4. **Today's parents** — 42
   Values
   Conflicting values

5. **Parenting roles** — 52
   Mothers
   Fathers
   Working mothers – where both parents work
   outside the home

6. **Learning and growing** — 61
   Opportunities for growth
   New people
   New places

7. **Learning for life** — 72
   Life skills
   Home skills

Contents

8. **Educational skills** 79
   Learning skills

9. **Starting school** 84
   Self-esteem at school
   Learning difficulties
   Visiting school
   Helping the school

10. **School days** 101
    Developing skills
    Judgement
    Adventure

11. **Friends and relationships** 111
    Differences
    Secrets and privacy
    Self-reliance
    Sex education

12. **Adolescence** 121
    Emotional change
    Finding identity
    Friendship
    Education

13. **Authority** 131
    Biblical authority
    Society and authority
    Family authority
    Under authority
    Challenges

14. **Establishing discipline** 141
    Limits reflecting parents' values
    Training for safety
    Communications
    Disobedience
    Tantrums
    Self-discipline

Contents

15. **Correction or punishment**   159
    Spanking
    Constructive correction
    Correcting in public
    Summary on how to correct behaviour
    Problems between children in the family

16. **Values and limitations in society**   169
    Advertising and television
    Food for health and growth

17. **Family work and leisure**   178
    Family leisure
    Family work
    Local community

18. **Children's fears**   190
    Dealing with fears
    Fear of separation

19. **Death**   194
    Being prepared
    The event
    The funeral

20. **Marriage breakdown**   199
    Lone parents
    Grief

21. **Expectations and problems**   209
    Expectations
    Abuse

22. **The gift of the family**   213

    Appendix   216

INTRODUCTION

To be a disciple of Jesus Christ is to seek to live out the principles of the Kingdom of God in all relationships – with people, with the environment, with work attitudes and lifestyles – in essence, to live the fullness of God's intention for humanity; an experience for which the whole of creation waits with eager longing. J. B. Phillips' translation of Romans 8 says that all creation waits 'on tiptoe' to see the sons of God come into their own.

Children have a special place in the heart of God. In Matthew 18 Jesus exhorts his followers not to despise these little ones, for in heaven their angels always behold the face of his Father. The love of parents for their children, deep, committed, self-sacrificing and enduring, is only a pale reflection of the love of the Father. But the love of parents is the gift of the heavenly Father to his children.

As the Holy Spirit is the gift of God for the life of the church, so too the Spirit permeates the life of the family that seeks to reflect the Kingdom of God in all its relationships.

Through teaching, preaching, study and fellowship the church becomes aware of the redeeming and renewing work of Christ in their midst; in similar vein, families are built up through reflecting on the principles that pertain to their life. The parents have a particular god-given calling; for they have the care of the dependent members of the family, to give more than they receive. Children receive more than they give, though in nurturing children for health, maturity and stability parents will increasingly be leading children also to give more than receive by the time they reach adulthood.

The shelves of popular bookshops and even newsagents stock a variety of books on child development and the care of children. Many advise parents on what to do about all the many things that may be wrong with children, or may go wrong soon, from illnesses and accidents to behavioural and emotional problems. As Christians we seek to live qualities of goodness, hope, love and encouragement with our children because we recognise that life itself emanates from God and parenting finds its fullest meaning in him. Christian parents are concerned to do more than solve problems as these arise, they seek to establish the full and rich life of the Kingdom among their family and for their children.

Through my own experience as a lone parent I came to know God more fully, and to realise the beauty of the relationship that God has with a child and the depth of his love and compassion for them. In my professional training and experience with children I realised how much the Holy Spirit is at work in the world to bring out the best for all children everywhere. To look forward to the coming of the Kingdom causes us to look for the fullness of human life for others in our roles as parents, teachers, Sunday School and Youth Leaders, as pastors and church members.

The responsibility for children is an awesome task. Doubts of our own ability to give without measure, or our fears of failure can loom large. Parents and others are not perfect, they do make mistakes, they fail to meet their own expectations, they have times when there seems no end or solution to the problems. But we live with the knowledge of the Cross and redemption of Christ. He came to bring all things together. In Ephesians chapter one, we find that God has made known to us his purpose and will, as a plan for the fullness of time, to unite all things in him. The fullness of the vision for our children is in God's hands and he will bring it to fruition. In the meantime our faithful response is to look forward to that time. That is our hope.

Parents need not be weighed down by their own shortcomings, but instead be aware that Christ through the Spirit is with them. Problems, even traumatic and bitter failures, may be offered to God for healing and redemption. All sin has been paid for on the Cross; confession, and the bringing of our failures and sins to Christ for redemption is to set sin aside. Do not oppress your family with your sense of guilt, that would be self-indulgent but find other ways through Christian fellowship and counsel to find assurance of forgiveness.

Paul's letter to the Ephesians says, 'For this reason I kneel before the Father, from whom his whole family in heaven and earth derives its name. [The Revised Standard Version says, "after whom every family in heaven and on earth is named".] I pray that out of his glorious riches he may strengthen you with power through his Spirit in your inner being, so that Christ may dwell in your hearts through faith. And I pray that you, being rooted and established in love, may have power, together

Introduction

with all the saints, to grasp how wide and long and high and deep is the love of Christ, and to know this love that surpasses knowledge – that you may be filled to the measure of all the fullness of God' (Ephesians 3:14–19).

With this as the background, parents should pray for their family life and for their children; that they may be strengthened with power through his Spirit that Christ may dwell among them; that being founded in love the family may grasp a sense of the unknowable love of Christ – that the fullness of God be among them.

The practical outworking of this knowledge of Christ in the family is seen in the new life Paul describes in Ephesians 4:22. The values that are taught for the church are for the family at home also. Children learn through what they experience at home, moral, ethical and spiritual values, so that we being concerned to teach these Kingdom values to our children should as the primary place of their learning, live those values in our families.

Parents, in addition to their own daily prayer relationship with God, should pray regularly for the family, for each other as parents, and for the children. There is no other way than with the power of the Spirit to see the establishing of the Kingdom, to see old patterns broken and renewed, to bring wholeness and healing. The renewal of life together requires being before God together, being open to him together, hearing him together and being obedient together.

The underlying philosophy of *Understanding Children* is that life itself is good. Despite the hard times and the struggles, the love, friendship, hope, and adventure that parents experience are well worth the cost.

Parenting is as full of excitement, disappointment, disaster and jubilation as any human experience can be. Relationships with children bring richness to marriage, not financially or in comforts, but in the intangible aspects of love and mutual care. The life of adults is enriched and matured as they give unstintingly to their children.

In the chapters which follow many parents will find that the ways they relate to children are affirmed. There are brief questionnaires in some sections to facilitate the reflection process; for opportunity to reflect specifically on aspects of child-rearing will enable readers to consider particular changes they would like to make. There are also questions for personal consideration at the end of each chapter.

This is an opportunity to re-evaluate family life with children, to reconsider old patterns and to challenge myths. It is to be expected that you will not agree with everything, so use your disagreement constructively, as an opportunity to define again how you wish to work with your children and why.

Above all, parents can believe in themselves and their love for their children, knowing that all parents make mistakes, most mistakes can be repaired and that those that are not readily repaired can be forgiven. The return for years of sacrificial care and nurture is not in material things but in the joy of the relationships, the friendship and the common enjoyment of life.

Most of us learn our parenting skills through what we experienced as children. In the past, society changed slowly and parents tended to repeat the patterns of their parents and others around them during their own childhood. However, contemporary society is changing rapidly and it is increasingly difficult for parents to simply copy any model, either from their own upbringing or from the local community. In this fast-moving environment, it is necessary for each generation to re-evaluate the principles and methods of parenting.

Reflecting on parenting, re-evaluating what we have done and what we do, helps us decide what we will do in the future. As we consider our past experience, how we grew up and the way we have parented so far, and as we *recognise* how change in society affects our parenting, we will better understand how much we go along with trends and how we might be different, if we want to be different.

A worthwhile prayerful preparation for a group of parents together, or other church groups working through this book, would be to read the scriptures from Ephesians 4:22–6:18, talking together briefly about members' experience of these in their own daily life. There are brief questions for group reflection given at the end of each chapter (as well as those for individuals) as many groups have found it helpful to look at aspects of the care and nurture of children together. While focused mainly on the role and work of parents, the material presented can help considerably in churches where members seek to support and encourage one another in their daily life and ministry.

To use the book as group study material I suggest the following:

– that each member of the group read the chapter at home, noting points of concern for themselves, points for clarification

and question. She/he should also answer the individual questions given;
– that the group have two leaders who are able to facilitate the study as well as to share themselves;
– that the group enable all members to speak, and respect and affirm all points of view.

Encouragement and hope bring new life, criticism and condemnation breed despair and hopelessness, as well as driving people away from the group. Don't forget that criticism can be disguised in superior attitudes so let no-one dominate from an 'I-know-it-all' position. He/she may have a lot of knowledge or experience, but its value to another parent's situation can only be assessed by that other parent.

When parents share their concerns, problems or failures in the group the leaders can use the creative problem solving approach (outlined later) as a means of encouraging parents to see that they have the means and grace to use the circumstances for good. Parents often feel as powerless in their own families as they do in the rest of their lives; a creative approach is needed to help them see that they have the power to make a difference. For leaders or others in a group to tell parents what to do and how to do it, only affirms and consolidates the powerlessness and makes failure more likely.

Chapters 18 to 21 have no group questions set. An established group of parents, or a church may benefit most in inviting those who work professionally with families with special needs, to speak to them on these topics.

The chapters of this book give only limited mention to several aspects of parenting that affect a minority of families. The amount written here about these is by no means relative to the needs of these groups but is an acknowledgement of the situation, to keep those of us not dealing with these aspects aware of the situations with which some parents are coping. Handicapped children with special medical and educational needs, as well as special care needs have barely a paragraph. They should have at least a book of their own. Similarly there is a slightly longer section on the Single Parent, touching on the issues with which they struggle. As a lone parent myself I was unaware of the issues and problems till I had to deal with them personally. I added this section to give awareness to two-parent families and assure the single parent there are sources of help of which they may not have been aware. The complexities of teenage life again are mentioned in the chapter on adolescence but parents of teenagers would be well advised to look at materials such as those published by the Open University for more particular study and reflection.

The book includes many short anecdotes of experiences with children. Their names have all been changed

1. ESTEEM AND RESPECT

At that time the disciples came to Jesus and asked, 'Who is the greatest in the kingdom of heaven?'

He called a little child and had him stand among them. And he said: 'I tell you the truth, unless you change and become like little children, you will never enter the kingdom of heaven. Therefore, whoever humbles himself like this child is the greatest in the kingdom of heaven.

And whoever welcomes a little child like this in my name welcomes me. But if anyone causes one of these little ones who believe in me to sin, it would be better for him to have a large millstone hung around his neck and to be drowned in the depths of the sea.' (Matt 18:1–6)

The disciples had asked Jesus about greatness and importance but he responded by talking about humility. A child was placed in their midst, a child who was unaware of his own humility. Jesus talked about welcoming children in his name and in doing so we welcome him. In the same way that Jesus in Matthew chapter twenty-five taught about the hungry, the thirsty, the stranger and the imprisoned, as those in whom the disciples would serve Jesus, here he gives a similar directive about their relationships with children. This serves as a background to understanding the development of self-esteem and respect in children; Jesus' concern for welcoming is brought into the broad principles of the effect of the ways in which we greet, speak, communicate and relate to children.

Everyone wants to feel special, to know they are uniquely recognised and accepted. It is the respect and affirmation of others that helps individuals grow to become secure, self-confident and interdependent adults. Eventually the fruit is in discovering an harmonious and full adult relationship with God.

What am I? Who am I? Am I important? Where do I fit into the world?

Discovering the uniqueness of his identity begins with the newborn baby. A child is born without any recognition of what is her body and what is the world around. The waving hands and feet are at first not recognised as her own movements as distinct from the mobile that hangs above the cot. Through simple discoveries – biting her finger hurts, biting the teddy's finger does not – the limits of the baby's physical existence are discovered. Taste, touch, sight, smell, and hearing are the sense through which the person begins to discover who he or she is.

At birth, a baby's world is constructed around their own needs. Basic physical needs overrule everything, even interrupting parents' sleep as the baby cries to be fed. By the time a baby reaches one year old she has begun to change, recognising other people to be as separate and alive as herself. She tries to control all the people around to suit herself. During the next few years she discovers gently and reassuringly, particularly with parents, that the world is a place of give and take and that the best relationships are those which are reciprocal. This understanding is the foundation of respect, for self and others.

By the time the toddler forms her first words and struggles to communicate with the people she meets, a lot has been discovered. Spoken communication has shown the child the difference between humans and other animals; the cat doesn't talk to people. There are attempts at conversation in which the child experiences herself more fully as a participant in family life. These foundational discoveries about self are the first steps on the path to understanding personal identity – physically, socially, and even spiritually.

Through the ways you relate to a child and to others in his presence, you teach a child to respect herself, yourself and those whom you respect. 'This person is special, care for him' will be communicated by your action, with or without your words. Later he can also understand, 'This person is special, God loves him.'

Consider the following statements: *Talking about a child in front of her is alright, she doesn't understand* – **False**. The child gets the message from the tone used and the manner of speaking. If the parent is being critical of the child, calling her a fool or implying that she is, the child takes that as a fair summary of herself and will expect little of herself. Even the child who is looking the other way, while swinging round an adult's feet, hears what is being communicated and will, from what she bears, have more or less self-respect.

Talking with a child about herself is helpful – **True**. Talk with a small child about his or her body and how it is the same or

Esteem and Respect

different from other bodies, about its size and shape. Compare straight and curly hair, childrens' bodies and adult bodies, brown skin and white skin, boys' bodies and girl's bodies.

Discover for yourself what you like and appreciate about your own body and what is fun about having a human body, what you can do and what pleases you. This is the same process of discovery for your child. Sharing your enjoyment helps her respect and cherish her own body.

Children should never interrupt an adult conversation – **False**. Adults interrupt one another so we can hardly expect our children to adopt what we don't keep ourselves. On the other hand, teaching respect and being respectful ourselves does mean helping children respect those who are talking; they ought not dominate the room with noisy disregard. Help children to listen and as they grow explain the subject of the conversation so they can join in.

If a child recognises or fears an emergency she should always interrupt. We may be glad she did. A hard and fast rule does not work, rather teach respect and tolerance for one another – even learning how to interrupt the conversation.

Children should share their toys with others – **False**. But they can learn to share at least some of the time. We all have treasures that we hold to ourselves. Dad has tools in the garage or shed and he restricts these for his own use; children have to ask his permission. Mum has make-up, paper and pens that she keeps for herself. Even a toddler can learn that there are items in a room that she is not allowed to have, that belong to others, that are not safe for playing.

Children also have treasures they keep for themselves. However, as childen grow, they invite others to play at home with them. It is good to encourage your child to share the toys she brings out while friends are there, or to leave in the cupboard the ones she would rather save for playing alone.

If *you* have invited another family with children to your house, talk with your child to find out which toys she is happy for the visitors to use. Occasionally, at times of insecurity, a child wants to share nothing. Do not violate this feeling, but collect your own toys from jumble sales and car boot sales to bring out when it's time for sharing. When she is ready and wants company your child will change.

When you make a sandpit in the garden, or put up a swing, you can explain to your child that this is a plaything that any one who is in the garden may use, it does not belong to them personally. When there are several children in the family this may be unnecessary as these are obviously family playthings, but for an only child the explanation is helpful.

Children shouldn't be forced to give presents – **True**. A present is a way to say 'I love you' or 'I like you', a gift from the heart. To receive a present that has been given out of duty does not make the recipient feel loved and cherished. It's better to wait until the child wants to join in gift-giving.

SELF-ESTEEM AND SELF-RESPECT – MESSAGES

Messages that we give to one another and to children build or break down their self-esteem. The messages we give and receive may be in words or may simply be in the non-verbal ways we relate to one another.

From the very first moments of life babies receive messages about themselves, messages in which words don't count, because they can't understand words anyway. Messages come through physical contact and everyday patterns of behaviour. Touch is a baby's chief way of receiving affirming messages. Cuddles and caresses, kisses and hugs tell the baby she is lovable, her body is good, Mum or Dad enjoys being with her. Taking even a few moments at bathtime to laugh with her as she kicks the water, tells your child you like what she does and you like being with her.

Esteem and Respect

There is strong cultural pressure to stop hugging and cuddling a child while he or she is still very tiny. The impression parents are given is that hugging a little boy will make him soft or sissy. The only ongoing form of touching affirmation given is in wrestling and play-fighting. Yet throughout a person's life he needs to experience affectionate touching from those close to him. Don't try to push a boy away or discourage him when he wants to be physically close to a parent. His feeling of being rejected may find expression as a continual demand for affection and attention.

As children grow, the ways in which a family expresses its love and appreciation for one another change. It also varies from person to person. Young children may enjoy the closeness of climbing into bed with their parents on Saturday or Sunday morning. They enjoy snuggling down together and talking, or even telling stories for each other. Older children may enjoy the physical contact of bearhugs and rough and tumble. A touch in passing or an arm round the shoulders expresses friendship and appreciation of one another. Teenagers often link arms with Mum or Dad as a sign of their affection, even though hugs may be unwelcome, or embarrassing.

Jesus expressed love and affection for others through touch. He healed many people through touching them. John the apostle is referred to in the Bible as the one who leaned on Jesus' breast; they showed their love and friendship for one another in physical closeness.

QUESTIONS FOR GROUPS OR INDIVIDUALS

Find a piece of paper and consider each of the following statements, writing down what you remember. In the last few days have you given or heard the following type of message being given? The words used may have been different, though the meaning was roughly the same, so write down the words you heard. You may wish to draw a small figure or character like ours but write your own words in the balloon.

1. 'I like you', or 'I enjoy being with you', or 'I love you'.

2. 'I like what you did', or 'That was well done', or 'I like the picture you painted'.

3. 'I know you could do better' or 'This is not good enough, I know if you tried again you could do better'.

All of these statements are encouraging and make the hearer more positive about herself. The first encourages the child to feel good about *who he or she is, the way she looks, her personality.*

The second statements encourage the child that *what she does is good and is pleasing to others, she can be pleased with herself.*

The third statement is a corrective statement that builds up the child. She is more *satisfied with herself* when she knows she has done a good job.

None of us is perfect. All of us have times of not bothering, letting things go poorly. Constructive and encouraging correction keeps the child *believing in her own ability and potential.*

There are biblical parallels to these messages which Jesus used. In the parable of the talents, two people who had done well were affirmed by the master. Jesus did not condemn the woman who had been caught in adultery or the rich young ruler, rather he received them as they were and sent them away with the knowledge that he believed they could do better.

Now consider the following three types of statements and again write down examples you remember from the last few days. You may have heard them or spoken them yourself.

4. 'You're so stupid,' or 'I wish you'd get out of the way' or 'It irritates me when you're here' or 'Must you do that?'

5. 'I suppose that's the best I can expect from you' or 'You always were a failure'.

6. 'You're not very good at reading, are you, dear?' or 'Shall daddy do that for you? It's rather hard, isn't it?'

These are the kinds of messages that break down our self-esteem and, despite our love for our children, we often find ourselves giving them. Around us is a world in which bad news is interesting, and honesty is often only thinly disguised criticism; it's no surprise that we find ourselves behaving negatively as well.

Message number four communicates to the child that she is the *wrong person, unwanted or unacceptable for the way she is;* the wrong shape, the wrong colour, or the wrong personality.

Number five tells the child that *she is a failure, she can't do the right thing*, and might as well not bother. If the child receives this message regularly she stops trying. Look again at message number three and see how that actually encourages the child to try again, and to try harder.

Message number six sounds good at first hearing but actually contains a subtle *'I-love-you-even-though-you're-a-failure'* message that builds up the parent but not the child. This message does not communicate hope and encouragement, it is sympathetic in a negative way that does not suggest the child can do better in future. A creative problem solving approach in the same situation, when an activity has not worked out well, would be far better.

After Easter, Jesus encouraged, affirmed and gave a fresh

start to his disciples. Peter had betrayed Jesus but he was not chastised but given new responsibility. Thomas doubted, so Jesus made a point of showing his hands, feet and side to Thomas. The two grieving disciples on the road to Emmaus had not understood the prophecies about Jesus despite all the teaching they had received, so Jesus spent time explaining the Scriptures again. He met all their shortcomings with patience, hope, redemption, and a fresh start.

Parents may inadvertently be breaking down self-esteem. But changes can be made from negative patterns.

Make yourself a simple diary or calendar for the next few days and each evening take a few moments to fill in some 'message' balloons. You'll find within a day or two that you are changing your messages to more affirming ones. You may even discover your family responding by giving you affirming messages also.

Only say what can be said with integrity, only when you mean it. Some children are unpleasant; they are hard to like, they seem always to be messy and unattractive. A major cause is the messages they have received throughout their life. A child who has heard many times that he or she is a nuisance or in the way is withdrawn and sheepish or even very demanding. Don't tell the child you like what she did if you don't. Instead, spend a little longer in reflection and, before you give a message, find *anything* you can to be positive about. Then look for another positive message. Try to cut down on the negative messages so you don't contradict your affirming words.

Not all our messages are in words. A child comes in with a painting she has done and Dad says 'Hmm' in a distracted sort of way. Later she sees the painting has been thrown in the bin, and the 'rejecting' message has come across loud and clear without words.

One small child I worked with in a playgroup programme had clearly interpreted the messages she had received. Jane was four years old but seemed unable to respond to 'Hello' or any other friendly exchange. She simply hid her face, either against her mother or put up her hands to hide herself. From her play it was possible to assess that she was of at least average intelligence; her problem was not that she could not understand. However, Jane seemed to most people an unpleasant child, she whined, mumbled, and snivelled, and her mother was constantly trying to stop this annoying behaviour.

We undertook a new way of relating to Jane, giving her

Esteem and Respect

different messages than she had previously heard, telling her we liked her activities. We smiled and encouraged her when she smiled back. Eventually she would respond with a cheery 'Hello' when we greeted her on her arrival with the other children. What Jane had needed was affirmation in the form of friendly exchanges throughout the day. She needed to know from the adults around her that she was good and we enjoyed her company and when we said 'Hello', we really were glad to see her. As she began to feel better about herself, her parents were able to see an attractive little girl whose company they enjoyed and their messages changed also.

The way we tackle our everyday activities may convey affirmation to build up self-esteem. Do children get the impression they are being hurried off to the next activity or place? Parents cannot spend time with them, they're too busy? You may have to walk home together, but afterwards, when you arrive home, do you choose to make a little time available to your child, so if he wants he can sit and talk, for no particular reason? It is at these kinds of moments or perhaps at bedtime, when there's time together, that a child shares her secrets or special discoveries with a parent. If you are always hurrying, the child feels instead that what is important to her is of no real importance to you and so will stop trying to tell her.

MUTUAL AWARENESS AND RESPECT

Small children are utterly ego centric, the result of being so vulnerable. A baby can meet none of her own needs; everything is done for her as she lie helpless. But because he or she starts off by needing someone to come when she cries, to do everything for her, she believes the world and all the people in it are hers to command.

Pay attention to your children. Find times to give them complete attention even for only a few minutes. I heard it said 'One minute of complete attention is worth a whole day of shared attention.' That's true. Talk with your child, listen to her. Take up some of the same interests together. Learn to swim when she does or go to watch her favourite sport with her and enjoy yourselves together.

Treat a child with the same respect that is shown to an adult, the respect that parents would like their child to show to them.

Do you have one way of talking to adults and one for children?

Parents may feel, or may have been taught as a child, that

adults are more important than children: the latter may be treated in a more dismissive way. Treating a child dismissively tells her that she is not worthy of respect and so affects her approach to life. In addition, when a child finds that parents are no more worthy of a pedestal than any other human being she may well despise them for setting themselves on one during her childhood. Look out for times when parents say things like 'Don't speak to your mother that way.' Are they suggesting that the child can speak to any other person, perhaps another child, that way? It might be worth trying a new approach: 'Don't speak to people like that; you hurt them.'

Children are people too, with rights and privileges just as important as those of adults. Respect their feelings. Sometimes a child does want to keep her feelings to herself. If she has told you how she feels don't betray the confidence any more than you would an adult confidence.

Some children seem to be tiny tyrants, but don't let them continue in this way. Help them to be more respectful of others before they get to playgroup and school or they may find it very hard to make friends. Children with older brothers and sisters soon learn it's no use trying to boss them around and a parent with several children doesn't usually have time to be at the beck and call of one. Circumstances help the necessary learning.

But for parents with only one child, help a bossy toddler to respect others. Don't let her hit you, or she will readily hit other children who will soon avoid her. Where there is more than one child in the family help them to respect each other's toys, asking before they play with a brother's toy. Don't let one child override another in conversations. Especially don't let a quiet child be overwhelmed by a more pushy brother or sister. Encourage children to listen to one another. It may be that while one child is talking, one of the others attempts to interrupt. Don't let the youngest monopolise the hugs or constantly interrupt.

Help children in their relationships with their friends. If they have hurt a friend, whether they meant to or not, help them learn the skills of reconciliation and of creative compromise. Talk about your own friendships and even of the ways you work out your differences as parents so that the child can see that forgiveness, compromise and saying sorry cement relationships together.

The Lord's Prayer gives a pattern of God forgiving us as we forgive one another. Often we have to ask him to help us

Esteem and Respect

forgive; our children can learn the same way in their friendships.

RESPONSIBILITY

Interdependence, freedom and responsibility are at one end of a scale while dependence and powerlessness are at the other. To be really free a person is fully responsible for himself and his relationships. A child, while immature, needs parents to look after her development and safety. She needs help in decisions and in communication with others. As she grows, however, she will increasingly be able to manage her life, to be independent, and eventually will live interdependently with others.

A baby needs caring adults who take full responsibility for her. Parents watch her, provide for her, and set safe limits within which she can play. Their care provides food and warmth, time to sleep, affection, and help. At appropriate times in a child's growth, she will learn to feed herself and take herself to the toilet. Later she will learn to cross roads, ride a bike and take herself to school.

From a very dependent beginning children grow to the stage of being able to maintain responsible, reciprocal, adult relationships.

Growth in forming friendships requires communication and negotiation with others. A child learns the patterns of conversation through listening and practice. As other people use words in their conversations with her the patterns and meanings become apparent. Recognition of self and of others comes through opportunity to converse. Learning to talk is first a question of hearing and listening. Someone talks to the baby often enough for her to realise that the words carry and reflect her parents' attitude to her, their plans for her and their own thoughts, ideas and feelings. Talk to your baby; explain what you are doing and why. Tell her what you think of her, especially your enjoyment in being with her. Tell the child that the dirty nappy smells and that you know how hungry she is. Have an on-going conversation with your child.

By eighteen months a child begins to join words together. Conversation is the goal. The child tries to negotiate with others and failing to do this with limited talking skills, she may have terrible tantrums. Although she has found the right words, she may fail to understand why everyone is not doing what she wants. At other times they find that despite trying their hardest, they cannot say what they want and will become extremely frustrated.

But taking responsibility for ourselves as adults involves 'being in charge of ourselves'. That requires us to consider feelings. Parents can talk to their child about their own feelings as they experience them. Tell the baby you are sad, delighted, or tired as it happens and he or she begins, having sensed your feelings anyway, to name feelings. As the parent expresses feelings the child learns to name and express her own.

When a child begins to express her own feelings with words, then she can learn to be in charge of herself without having to deny or repress those feelings. She learns to be angry without hurting others; to be sad without making others run round after her to make her feel better; when she is bored or fed-up to say sorry that she has hurt others through her bad-temperedness. Moods in people of all ages are strong feelings that control the individual without their being able to talk to others about them or cope with them creatively. It is not a question of trying to make the feeling go away, but of handling oneself in the midst of it.[2]

A child who comes in bad-tempered from school each day is liable to hit out in rage. Help by asking how school has been today; ask how he or she feels.

When a child has pent-up feelings try *active listening*. This enables them to say what they want, and to be heard and received without judgement. Here's a simple technique to start you off, using an example that proved extremely helpful to my next door neighbour and her son.

Ask a question such as 'Have you had a good day?' Let your child respond however she wishes, for example, 'That's a silly question!' **Do not ask another question**, but respond in a way that tells your child you are listening. Say to her, 'You think that's a silly question?' Use words similar to the ones they used. The child will then say more about her feelings and thoughts. Reassure her you're listening by using a fairly repetitive statement that does not interpret her words but simply repeats them. Though at first you may feel rather like a parrot, this technique encourages the child's expression and your listening. With time the child sorts and interprets her own responses without you saying much at all.

A child often feels guilty when an activity doesn't work out as she planned or expected. Taking responsibility is not the same as taking the blame in a guilty and limiting way. Try

Esteem and Respect

saying 'If you were going to start again, what would you do differently?' The child then begins to look back to consider other possibilities and alternatives. Why did this project not turn out as planned? Could she have done something differently? Guilt can result in a bitter experience without positive learning. Reflection can result in a positive lesson being learned, turning guilt to constructive reconsideration of the problems. Just as a parent may ask himself, 'Why did it not work this time, when it did last time?', the child grows to consciously reflect and learn from experience. Such reflection is not a time for pushing a child into adult attitudes but to facilitate following through on her own thoughts. The problems she faces, whether during construction with wood or in games with friends, can be tackled creatively.

Opportunity to make decisions helps a child grow to maturity. There are decisions that affect only the child, what she plays with, or how she spends her time or uses tools. The child who is seven plus should have opportunity for personal decisions. She should have an environment which requires her to make decisions, encouragement to take responsibility and to go ahead with her choices. Allow the child responsibility over toys and pocket money, things over which she can take complete control. But remember, don't be tempted to interfere once you've let them have responsibility. Let her find out how she likes to spend her money. Don't suggest that she can have her cake and eat it too; if the child spends all her money on the first day, then let her be without for the rest of the week.

There are decisions that a child makes which affect other people. When a child is choosing a birthday treat ask if she thinks the guests or the rest of the family would enjoy choice. She may well hesitate, thinking about her friends, then quite happily adapt her ideas to something she knows they would like too.

The responsibility for a pet can encourage a child, though you should check she follows through and feeds an animal consistently and adequately. Since the care of an animal such as a dog or cat has to happen every day, regardless of the novelty having worn off, and goes on for a number of years, the whole family has to be prepared for the demands of a pet. Consider, before acquiring the pet, that you know how it will be cared for when you go on holiday; that you can get to the vet and afford the bill if the animal is sick; that someone is going to walk a dog every day.

Children reaching their teens should be able to cope with

their own travel. Be sure the child has the skill to cope with reading a timetable, or for asking the ticket inspector or bus conductor for help. Look out for the pitfalls and assess realistically what your child can cope with and let her tackle many new situations; if a child is used to looking for her own creative solutions to problems she will be reasonably safe.

The young adult has learned to think and take responsibility for herself. She knows what she thinks, what she feels and how her decisions may affect others. At this stage parents are friends, those to whom the young woman can say 'I know what I think and I know what I feel. I can see several choices. I want to hear what you think. Then I will decide.' Such freedom does not mean that the young adult can expect to get everything she wants. Many choices are hard or unpleasant.

There always are decisions which a person would make differently if she could turn the clock back. However, do not deny a child the opportunity to make decisions and be responsible for herself, though she may be hurt or uncomfortable in the process.

The opposite of freedom is powerlessness. A child who has no sense of involvement in the decisions of her daily existence is like a mechanical train on someone else's track. She can be stuck in a pattern of demanding that others meet her needs, complaining and nagging when they don't. Reflection and choice are elements in the growth to responsibility, and a parent should avoid manipulation, punishment or open frustration while a child learns to choose for herself.

Consider the following list of responsibilities and fill in a list for each of your children.

Skills:
Knows how to cross the road with the crossing lady.
Can ask for goods and get change.
Knows the value of coins if helped.
Can make sandwiches.
Can set the table.
Can wash up.
Can use the vacuum cleaner.
Cooks if parents deal with the oven.
Add further examples for your own child

Responsibilities:
Has pocket money of her own.
Cleans and tidies up own toys and belongings.

Esteem and Respect

Tidies own room on Saturdays.
Occasionally chooses and makes Saturday tea for the family.

These examples could be for an average eight-to-ten-year-old. For each of your children consider what responsibility you would like them to be able to handle in a year's time and then list the skills they would need in order to take that responsibility. Provide them with the opportunity to learn those skills.

Sometimes circumstances provide ideal opportunities for learning new skills. Help them with the skills needed so that when the time comes they are not too afraid or helpless.

QUESTIONS FOR INDIVIDUALS OR GROUPS

Looking back over this chapter consider the following questions, making yourself a note of your responses.
1. Remember a person or incident in your own childhood when you felt especially affirmed. The event may have been at home or at school, with friends or relatives.
2. Remember an occasion, or occasions, when as a child a mistake you made turned out badly; you still feel badly about it. What was the response of the adults, or your parents? If you kept it a secret, why did you?
3. What things did you most appreciate about your parents and family life? Are there certain times or events that stick in your memory as being special?
4. Note particular times of sadness or difficulty. Were you able to tell anyone your feelings; did someone understand? Who?

If you told no-one, was it because you wanted to keep your feelings to yourself, or that you felt no-one cared?
5. Are there ways in which you could give your child more responsibility?

QUESTIONS FOR GROUPS

1. Read together Isaiah 43:1–7. Reflect on this passage. How precious is each person to God? What kind of message does this passage suggest he would like people to hear?

Look at Isaiah 44:1–5. Consider how God will bless the offspring and descendants of his people.

How do these passages throw light on the nature of God's love? Read again Matthew 18:1–6. In what terms would you describe God's love for children?

2. Consider the settings in which as a group you are together with children. (This may be in church, in a playgroup, in school, or on social occasions.)

Do adults include children in their conversations? Or is there a tendency for adults to carry on their own conversations while trying to stop children interrupting?

Do you, or can you, make opportunity to talk to each other *and* to one another's children?

3. Look over the section on messages again. Talk about the kinds of messages you give and receive, in your group, in your families, in your church, and other settings.

4. In your settings, whether a child-centred group such as school or playgroup or a wider group such as church, are there opportunities for children of all ages to take responsibility? If there are too few, can you make or recommend changes?

Footnotes

[1] *Self-Esteem, A Family Affair* by Jean Illsley Clarke (Winston Press 1978) has several sections on 'strokes' or positive and affirming messages.

[2] The books of John Powell are of interest to those who wish to understand more about feelings and their expression.

2. SPIRITUAL DEVELOPMENT AND THE CHURCH

Children are received into the church as babies, in a variety of ways that reflect our denominational understandings. For some there is the sacrament of baptism, for others there is a service of dedication. Whichever we have chosen for our children we are concerned to understand and nurture their faith in God and to develop their relationship to the church as God's people in the most creative way.

SPIRITUAL GROWTH

From the time of conception a child is a spiritual being, for that is the nature of human life. The person's relationship to God, in which spirituality is expressed, is first a gift from God. St John in his first epistle said that we love because he first loved us. In the same epistle, John addressed himself to several groups within the church, the little children, the fathers and the young men. To the little children he writes, 'because you know the Father' (1 John 2:12–14).

How can we begin to understand a child's relationship to God, and her spirituality which is the expression of that relationship? How can we as parents nurture the child's relationship to God and how can the church include children?

A child finds her own identity as she is loved, protected and provided for by her parents. The appropriate relationship between parent and child is first for the parent to give and the child to receive. It is a giving that is unconditional: the baby receives gratuitously, her response is enjoyed and appreciated but not demanded. The child is not rejected when she fails to smile or please her parents, or if she cries when this is inconvenient to them.

So too with God. The love of God is expressed to the child through people, the parents, the family, friends and neighbours, the church. Being loved is an essential foundation to being able to give love in return. All the aspects of affirmation, respect, appreciation, and friendship that are given to a child help towards her own mature, adult response to God in later years.

The whole of creation is an expression of God, and reflects his life to a child. The wind, the sun, the clouds and rain, light and dark, are immediate experiences for a child. The richness of her experience introduces the child to the richness of God, though a small child will not recognise these as God-given. A child who has never seen or touched a mountain or the sea will have no ability to appreciate those as expressions of God's creativity. So as children grow, the richer their experience of God's creation, the greater can be their sense of wonder at the majesty and power of God.

The child's ever-widening experience through home and school introduces her to greater potential for appreciating the diversity and creativity of God. It is in this light that the chapters of this book on many aspects of a child's life and development are written. In learning to read or to study mathematics a child is uncovering the beauty of the order of created life, that is both full of pattern yet, like a kaleidoscope, open to endless possibilities.

These are the raw materials of spirituality, those which the child receives and in response to which she can grow up to give in return.

For a child to respond to God in worship, thanks and service, there are many ways in which parents and other adults may nurture the spirituality of the child, help her to an expression of faith appropriate to her age and understanding.

The many aspects of daily life and of relationships, where love and creation are continuing experiences that the child meets, are covered in other chapters, but in this chapter we cover those aspects that enable a child to respond and perceive God as Father and Creator, the one in whom life finds its meaning. These are the spiritual aspects of life, for spirituality encompasses all of life as a quality in which the rest of life is contextualised.

PARENTS AND FAMILY

Parents offer a very special committed love to a child, a love that is peculiar to their relationship, and at the same time expresses particular aspects of God's love to the child.

Spiritual Development and the Church 27

Often we see that when another person, friend or acquaintance, holds the baby she enjoys the baby's smiles and gurgles. Then the baby is sick, or its nappy begins to leak, so the friend hands the baby back to the parent. When the baby is sick, distressed, screaming, unpleasant, unbearable, unattractive, messy or smelly the parents are those who unconditionally hold onto her, cherish and comfort her. While others may at times offer expressions of love, in such circumstances their gift is temporary, whereas parents have chosen, in having a child, to give without measure. This is the same love that Christ offered all creation. In his act of taking on human form and being killed, he expressed the unconditional love of God in the everyday human situation.

In the family a child begins to glean her first understanding that God is the source of life, and of love and of creation, through seeing and hearing the family relationship to God. Their prayers offer thanks to God for the goodness around them. The family prays about the problems of daily work and living so the child is aware of God's concern for the concerns of the family.

A family has opportunity to tell Bible stories to a child. As a history of God's people, they are relevant to the family in the same way as recollection of its recent history is found by looking through family albums. These help a child know her roots, heritage, descent and identity. She hears about grandparents, and about her parents' marriage and commitment to one another and to God. The Bible is therefore no ordinary story. Through hearing the story of God's people through the ages a child grows in her sense of the larger family and people to which her own family belongs.

Often parents ask me whether a child is confused by hearing stories about God in the same way they hear stories that are fiction. Consider: a child hears in story that there are fairies at the bottom of the garden. The child also hears a story about trees at the bottom of the garden. The child quite sensibly decides that the trees are real and the fairies are not, and so dismisses the latter. Why do they do this? They see through both the actions and conversations of their parents that the trees are taken seriously but the fairies are entirely ignored with regard to real life. The child leaves the latter as part of fiction. Similarly, a childhood belief in Father Christmas is eventually discarded. But as a child experiences that her parents seriously regard the reality of God, she will not dismiss the nativity along with the fictional Faather Christmas. On the other hand if parents are not taking the nativity seriously then the child learns from them to disregard this aspect of the incarnation of Christ. Children learn from what parents do more than from what they say.

Family Prayers
For some families a regular Bible reading and a prayer from one of the family, either at breakfast or tea-time is a helpful form of family prayers. Other families find it more constructive to follow set forms and use readings set for each day from Bible notes or a lectionary. Whatever works for your family, as a way of expressing your worship to God, and as a means of summarising your relationship to him, is the best form for you to use. So experiment to find what suits you.

I have now encountered several families and communities who have found helpful liturgies from more unusual sources. The Jewish traditions have longstanding liturgies for everyday use. The liturgy for the Sabbath eve (Friday evening) is very beautiful. I am aware that this form has changed little from the one that Jesus himself would have used each Sabbath eve with his family and with his disciples. It is simple enough for any family to use, including the lighting of a candle, prayers of thanksgiving, and sharing of bread and wine.

A family could use this either on Friday as a thanksgiving for the week that is past, or on Saturday as a preparation for the Christian Sabbath.

There is no merit in setting up an arduous form for daily prayers in the family. Jesus pointed this out to the Pharisees who specialised in making hard work out of worship, as if this would earn them credit with God. Rather Jesus suggested that the people pray simply, and to this end taught them the Lord's Prayer.

If it is hard to hold your child's attention you may find it helpful to use simple set forms, then the child will learn to repeat the prayers with others. Light a candle as a focus for the time of worship, to create a special atmosphere, or use other visual signs that suggest that this time is special.

Family prayers give an ideal opportunity to prepare children for going to church.

CHURCH AND FAMILY

A service of worship is the time when the people of God in that church meet together to worship and hear him together.

Spiritual Development and the Church

Being part of such an event is an essential element in the nurture of a child's faith. Among God's people a child hears of God's goodness, experiences God's word among his people, finds love and acceptance, joins in worshipping God, and takes part in the people's faithful response to God's call.

Under-threes. The primary gifts that the church has for tiny children are those of belonging to the church and of unconditional love. The affectionate welcome as a friend, the tolerance, the patient sharing of books, and encouragement to participate, are all expressions of the church's nurturing of small children. This child's appropriate response to God is to be in the midst and be a recipient of these.

Three-to-Six-Year-Olds. Through the years of playgroup and infant school a child is beginning to feel a sense of the group and wants to be included in its activity. While a baby is content to have her needs met from a caring adult, with lots of personal love and affection, the growing child now wants to be part of the game, the family meal or social occasion.

The will is there but the skills may not be. When a game is played the child may actually disrupt the order of it. But she does not want to go and play something alone or with an accompanying adult. During this time also they begin to play with their peers instead of simply playing their own game alongside them. The group activity is the focus.

Within the family setting the child now wants to take part in family prayers and bible story times. Find ways for them to participate in a meaningful way, that does not however reduce the family prayers to being children's prayers. Parents should pray about the things that concern them as well as helping the child present her own prayers. With help, a child can light or blow out the candles and help set the table or call everyone together for prayers. If a set form is used she could be in charge of handing out and putting away the books.

During family prayers encourage even a small child to be quiet to listen to others. Just as respect in any conversation is a learned attitude, so respect in worship can be learned in the family. For a three year old to be still and quiet for a brief silence or during the prayers of others, one parent's full attention may need to be given to helping them take part.

Recognising a child's wish to participate in the group activity, the service can be structured and planned with emphasis on the congregation's participation. Help the child to be still to listen (just as someone's attention was given to this at home so it will be in church); sit in the front seats so they can see all that happens, especially for 'eventful' services such as the Communion service. Make sure that the stewards know the child's name and help her say hello to them, collecting a book like others of all ages; this gives her a sense of being a member of the corporate event and activity. Encourage the child to sing when others sing, even when they don't know the words, to kneel when others kneel to pray, to be silent when others are silent.

Avoid the pitfall of creating a Children's service. Plan all-age worship, for then children are nurtured through being among a worshipping people; it does little for them to be the focus of the service, when the purpose of a worship event is to focus on God.

This rudimentary sharing in the group, both church and family, is an expression of the child's spirituality at this age, as a dependent member of the church, having no separate and distinct life of their own. Just as her everyday life is maintained by her parents and family, so her response to God is dependent of others. If those around express no worship to God the child does not.

Six-to-Twelve-Year-Olds. Many basic skills of language and

Spiritual Development and the Church 31

negotiation are thoroughly established by the time a child is six or seven. Often they can read quite fluently, can follow instructions, can think out plans and schedules, and be happy to serve others in order to gain a common objective. She often happily curtails her own plans to fit in with other people, but is discouraged if the group does not give her an opportunity to be creative and expressive.

This age-group seems to thrive more than any other on a creative approach to church worship. The child can quickly become distracting and destructive if the church expects them to be present as audience not participant. But given the chance to participate the child can be wholehearted and generous. Eight to twelve year olds volunteer their help in music, drama, prayers, and dance, as acolytes and stewards. To adults who are more complicated and subtle in response to God, the child's involvement may seem too naive. Yet often the child has a faith in God's goodness and love that is remarkably trusting and straightforward. God does answer the prayers of children, so their trust is not ill-founded; God receives their worship.

A church that establishes a worship service for all ages, that recognises that worship is, by definition, essentially an act of participation in an encounter with God, can give any immeasurable amount to children of these ages. It's gift to children is in making a way open for children to give their response to God along with the rest of the congregation. The child will not be satisfied with a children's slot in the service, for that implies that the child is there to receive when really she is nurtured most through giving.

Those who lead worship for all ages, with a concern for the nurture of all members, will then be looking for structures, forms and liturgies that facilitate the worship of everyone present, in an all-age worship service.

Teens. The teenager should have the opportunity to discover and assert for herself the foundational direction of her life. She is able to participate as an adult in the life of the church, and able to take responsibility for her own prayer and worship life. The spiritual task of the teenager includes discovering for herself whether she is going to take up the responsibility of discipleship and how to follow God's call on her life. Where parents have, till now, been responsible for the child's life and growing knowledge of God this now becomes her own responsiblity.

In the family there may be tensions. It may become hard work to maintain family prayers. The younger child wanted to belong and participate in the group activity, she may now experiment with not participating. In this transition from dependence to personal responsibility it is not necessary for the family to give up their prayers together. For this, in an indirect way, presents their own life values as a continuing expression of faithful worship in the family. If may be less distracting to their continuity if the family uses a set liturgy rather than depending on spontaneous offerings, and make prayers optional to the teenager though requiring her to respect them. For example, if the family is used to saying a prayer before supper, this can continue and the teenager who chooses not to take part in the prayer would not begin to eat, nor cause distraction while others are praying. Both family and individual can respect the differences.

Most churches with active teenage members find their nurture is best served with a youth group or youth leader. Teenagers have particular questions and responses to consider, and are helped by having someone with whom they identify, and a group to go to, in which such questions can easily be asked without embarrassment. Both teenagers who are more committed and those who are 'anti-church' can find their help in this group.

As young people begin to take up responsibility for their own spiritual lives, the church should ensure there is room for them to give and serve, taking responsibility in its life. There should be opportunity to be responsible in worship and in the church's caring ministry. People who are discovering their own maturity as individuals either find access to being active responsible members of the church or they find the church to be empty of meaning and unrealistic.

Each person has a God-given identity, having a special place in his heart. Through the people around them and through their daily experience, children receive life from God. As parents and the church give them the opportunities appropriate to age so children grow in faith, knowledge and fellowship with God. Children grow in spirituality, from complete dependence, being receivers of love, to being those who want to give along with everyone else, till eventually they can take responsibility for themselves and become disciples.

QUESTIONS FOR INDIVIDUALS AND GROUPS

1. The priority that the family gives to the things of God tells the child about the relative importance of God to the family.

Spiritual Development and the Church

If the family serves God at their own convenience, then the child will imitate these values.

Consider the priorities in your own family life. Are there points at which you would like to make changes? You may wish to talk these over with your partner and other family members.

2. Read through Psalm 139. Consider God's care for each person. Note the extremes to which he goes.

All parents are tempted at times to give up and fall short of this love. What do you consider are the points at which you have failed and would like to make a fresh start?

You may find it helpful to talk this question over with a friend. Making a fresh and more positive start is always easier when someone else is encouraging and helping you.

QUESTIONS FOR GROUPS

1. Tell each other your responses to the individual questions above.
2. In addition tell each other how you have tried, succeeded or failed with family prayers. Pool ideas and suggestions so each family can share the fruit of others' experience. Remember all families are different and those outside can offer ideas but not prescriptions.
3. Consider the worship services in your church. Are the children of all ages welcome to worship with everyone else?

Do you think the church members are aware of the importance of children being able to worship with everyone else? Is some action necessary?

Do you have ideas about the services and how a child's relationship with God could be more effectively nurtured in the church?

Can you invite one or more of your worship leaders to your group to discuss your thoughts and ideas with you?
4. Discuss ways to assess whether parents are fulfilling Christian principles in the way they live so that children are seeing life with Christ at the heart. For example, (and you can find other questions to discuss that fit your setting) is the family willing to give generously to some kinds of people only, or does the family give freely to all, regardless of class, religion, colour, creed, age etc? Is open house really true only for friends and those who are alike?

3. A CHILD'S VIEW OF LIFE

Just as a baby cannot tell where her hand ends and the teddy bear begins, she cannot see a relevant difference between what she imagines and what is concrete around her. Fantasy and reality are freely mixed in the child's view of life.

When a child is doing something concrete, whether as a play project, in a relationship, or in a conversation, he is working in reality. What she anticipates, thinks of or dreams up, is fantasy until it happens. Interaction with people and things is reality. An adult normally knows the difference; often a child does not.

Disappointments and frustrations for both adults and children stem from finding that the gap between fantasy and reality cannot be bridged. We have a strong imagination, a clear expectation of what will happen, and it doesn't. Every person should have enough positive experiences to want to work with reality. But it is crucial that we also hold onto fantasy, our ability to imagine and dream, to aspire to what is as yet beyond us. We bring together our ambitions with the reality of our actual skills and abilities, our romantic dreams with the reality of our loved ones, our inventions with the tools and materials we have.

Every time we say 'If only I had . . .' we are working with fantasy as opposed to reality. This reflection that uses our imagination helps us say, 'If I had the same circumstances again, I would . . .' and begin creative problem solving.

Integrating of fantasy and reality in a life process begins in the child. Most Pre-School age children do not clearly differentiate between fantasy and reality. A well known children's story book about a lion in the garden[1] is an illustration that the imagined or dreamed lion is to be feared and dealt with seriously. As children grow they are more readily able to sort out real things from things imagined. Talking to others and comparing experience helps that differentiation happen. Even as adults all of us need to talk to others or we can be over-

A Child's View of Life

whelmed by what we imagine, whether in romance, a nightmare, or a false picture of our importance.

Many small children have an imaginary playmate, often talked about to the adults around. To the child the playmate is real and a good companion. Do not try to force the child to 'see reality'. Allow their natural inner growth to lead them to choosing friends who are more tangible. Imaginary playmates have usually 'departed' by school age, of the child's own volition. The child's daily discoveries help the integration. When a child has realised that the lions in England all live in zoos, she realises for herself that the lion she saw in the garden was probably not 'real'.

It is helpful to children if parents are very honest when they ask questions about reality. If a parent leaves the family, don't pretend he's coming back. If grandmother dies don't make up a story of where she has gone. Children are able to know the truth.

Everyone, children included, has images that seem to come from the subconscious mind. Carl Jung, the psychologist, talked of the collective subconscious and archetypes to describe the phenomenon of the pictures that it seems the majority of people hold, especially when dreaming. There is no apparent external experience that gives those pictures. Things are imagined that have never existed. Sometimes it is a beast or person, sometimes a circumstance that is remembered more often when frightening. But all people have some kind of pictorial representation of things that come from deep within them and are very important.

When talking with children about God, I found many of them pictured God in very particular ways. It seemed that the human race has given 'shapes' to strong forces of good and evil. The fight between good and evil and the ultimate victory of the good is presented in many folk tales and legends. Children automatically identify with and want to hear these ancient stories of knights and dragons, of good and evil, often wanting them over and over again.

Hearing these fairy tales and folk stories enables children to externalise their own pictures of good and evil and resolve some of the inner tensions that go with them. When in the darkness of their own mind they sense something evil they can recognise it in the story, and can experience their own 'dragon' being killed or punished. Stories help them contain and resolve their own inner fantasy.

Hearing of the child's daydreams, others grow to understand

them. A child who feels the odd one out in the family often imagines that she is really a princess and one day her real parents will discover her and take her home. Fairy tales of princesses are of special interest. Eventually the child realises for herself that she is neither odd nor a princess in hiding but for the meantime she has had a fantasy that has helped her cope with her own feelings. Such dreams and fantasies are incredibly important to a child. They must not be violated. Do not laugh at them. Treat these as real feelings for that is what the stories represent symbolically. Encourage and help the child who dreams of being a princess, but do not tamper with the dream for that is her way of coping with her strong feelings. Only time will help her cope differently.

Contemporary studies of personality show that certain personality types are very likely to feel the odd one out at home and at school.[2] Affirmation can help a child feel accepted for who she is, though for a long time that no one really knows her. Probably she feels she is right, because there may be no one around her who thinks like she does or tackles life in quite the same way.

It follows then that as fantasy is often a sign of deep inner expressions of a person, that a child's fantasy should be considered with care and understanding. Receive a child's feelings and dreams in the same way; be an active listener and give the child time to process her thoughts and feelings herself in the context of the reality she experiences.

All of us at various stages of our lives, not only as children, have various pictures, mental images or visions of God; that's part of our human nature. Such pictures do not define God, but reflect our human desire to give a tangible, comprehensible shape – a way of naming God within the confines of human experience. Hence we have a picture of God as Father, when the reality of being God means he is immeasurably greater than any human father, so different that the comparison hardly stands. Even Elijah, who asked to see God, did not see God, but saw the glory of God, the weight of the presence of God.

THE POWER OF PARENTS

Parents are the most important people in a child's life. They are the source of life in a child's experience. With them she experiences the mutual love and affection that bring human fulfilment. The child's life comes from its parents at conception. she is nurtured and protected inside the body of her mother

A Child's View of Life

and when born, would die if all needs were not met by parents. As important as the physical needs are the emotional ones; the need to feel loved is met in being held, cuddled and caressed. The child who does not bond emotionally with her parents at birth is noticeably at a disadvantage as she grows.

Being in such a relationship to a child gives the parents enormous power and responsibility. They can make life good or bad for a child. These foundational experiences determine the child's attitude to herself, other people and to life itself. A person's attitude to God is affected similarly. A child who knows that life is good, on the basis of her experience, is more able to conceive of a God who is good. A child for whom life is negative and unloving more readily dismisses the idea of a loving God.

The parents are, for their child, the first tangible expression of the love of God. If they are overbearing, domineering, cruel, dishonest, manipulative, or emotionally distant, a child approaches future relationships and beliefs with the expectation that these qualities lie behind the words and actions of others. In contrast if she experiences hope, trust, honesty, openness, forgiveness, and reconciliation in her parents she has this expectation of her experience of life. The problems of daily life are treated as obstacles to overcome rather than signs of hopelessness and despair.

Children believe what they experience. Each person interprets new experience into the already established picture they have of life. An act of generosity can be interpreted as a hint that the recipient is not good enough, because of the attitude of the recipient to themselves. Affirmation, respect, treating the child as a person of infinite value, creates in her a hopeful attitude and belief in the goodness of life.

Does a parent have to become a paragon of virtue, presenting all that is good to a child? The truth is, none of us are. We try and we fail. At our weakest points we are defensive and hide from our own inadequacies. If we are critical of our child, we think *she* has a problem. Whatever her shortcomings, our negative attitudes are based on her not meeting our fantasy or projection of what she should be. Maybe parents who are very clever with their hands have a child who is less well co-ordinated, so they find fault with her. To love the child for who she is, the way God made her, is to open up ways for her to develop herself and her own giftedness.

RELIGIOUS BELIEFS

Children are growing towards making their own choices. Being responsible means making her own choice, living with that choice and if necessary reconsidering and remaking the decision. There is no bypassing this process on the way to maturity. Teenagers spend time examining the meaning of life and their beliefs, or lack of them, in God. A child will go through many thoughts and feelings as she decides for herself. Being responsible for herself also means that she will not automatically reproduce the values and beliefs of parents or the older generation unless as a result of her own choice. The result is the integrity of the young adult taking responsibility for herself, not from unthinking repetition. Often the values of parents and children do turn out to be fairly similar.

When parents have strongly held beliefs, and, for example, have experienced their faith in God helping them through hard times in their life, the choice their child makes brings out all sorts of feelings, not least of which is fear. They may be afraid that she may never find faith if she doesn't go to church. They may be anxious that she will choose standards that they know to be immoral. They may be worried about the child's future, either that without God's guidance she will have a bad time or that eventually she may not go to heaven. They may be hurt that their child is rejecting their values, and in some way not trusting their word about God. All these are very real and normal feelings for parents to have. Most parents sacrifice a great deal for their children and feel the investment they have made in the child is very significant. The prospect of losing such potential feels terrible. But the time comes to take the risk that all the hope and love that parents have given their children will ultimately be valued for what it is. Parents have to take a risk and trust their child to make a good decision, as she perceives it, even if it is different from their own.

What makes it so extremely hard to let our children make their own choice about faith?

Historically, we get the impression that a strong sense of duty to parents resulted in children following their parents more closely in the past than today's children. Maybe, maybe not. But we can still feel very guilty ourselves if our children don't do what we think we should be making them do. Sometimes grandparents, fearing the wilfulness of young people today, put emotional pressure on parents to raise children differently. Sometimes parents are afraid they will be discredited in their own church if their children appear to be 'dropping out'.

Spend some time reflecting on the principles above; it is more important for parents to be settled about what they are doing with their children than for other relatives or even church members to be satisfied. If they are neglecting their children or being cruel to them it would be good if the neighbours did intervene. But if they are merely fearing outside disapproval, it could be that they are wrong.

Doesn't the Bible say, 'Spare the rod and spoil the child.' But aren't you going against it by saying they should have a choice?

All young children need limits around them to protect them, to give them a safe place for learning basic life skills, to have time to grow into responsibility. It would appear from the words quoted that spanking was an acceptable way of setting limits, but like many other customs of biblical times, that is not particularly acceptable today.

QUESTIONS FOR INDIVIDUALS AND GROUPS

1. Think about yourself and consider your strong points: *What are you like?* (circle the characteristics you think fit you) shy, relaxed, flamboyant, quiet, outgoing, friendly, worried, timid, aggressive, bossy. (Write in any other words that would more aptly describe you.)

   What are your practical skills? (circle those you are good at and write in others) sewing, cooking, woodworking, writing, interior design, gardening? *What are you like socially?* a good host or hostess, easygoing, correct. *What are your bad points?* (some of the qualities you have circled above may be ones you think of as bad points. List those and any others here.)

   Go slowly back through this list deciding why you think each quality is bad. What can you do to change any of these or your attitude to yourself?

2. Think about your child and the good things you see in him or her. Write down the qualities you like.

   Consider whether you are doing all you can to encourage the good points and develop your child's own strengths. Underline aspects that you could encourage her to develop more.

   Friends are the best people to reflect back to parents their negative attitudes to their own children and even to help them see their children in a different light. Sit down with a good friend and ask her the following questions: What are the good things you see in me as a friend? What am I good at? What are my weak points?

   Her picture will be different from yours, but since she does appreciate you as a friend, you can expect the experience to be affirming. Ask the same friend how she sees your child. Any bad point will be less significant than the way you see it and your friend will almost undoubtedly be able to see the points at which you unintentionally discourage your child. Choose a trusted friend who would not put you down for your weakness. If she tells you that you are just a bit of a snob, and to you that's a weakness, think about whether you can change. If you can't, reflect on how you can cope with who you are and not hurt your child by imposing expectations that are, as a result, too high.

3. Take time to reflect on your own faith. Why do you believe in God? Do you believe because your parents did, or can you list the experiences that encouraged you to believe?

   What have been the most helpful influences on your faith,

A Child's View of Life

your own inner conversation with God, your friendships, your church? Think how each has helped you.

4. Make a summary of your child's religious beliefs as you see them. Are they still holding a very simple faith, dependent on your own faith, or have they moved on to look at questions of faith for themselves? As you see the progression she is working through, you will be more able to allow her to do it without your intervention, however lovingly. Remember that the faith she has at the end will be much stronger for having come to it herself.

QUESTIONS FOR GROUPS

1. Read the story of the child Samuel in 1 Samuel 1:1–2:11, 18–26; 3:1ff. The story of Samuel as a child faithful to God, is a very well-known story. As a group note down the ways in which you think he was an unusual child. What is your estimate of his age when God spoke to him? What form would you expect that Eli's care took, since the boy was visited once a year by his mother? List any other children in the Bible to whom God spoke, or were anointed for a special calling, while still a child.

2. Spend time listening to one another's response to the individual questions. Be cautious in offering answers or advice as members talk, most parents are in a process of discovering themselves as Christian parents and feelings hurt or criticised by the group could do more harm than good.

3. What have been important times of choice for group members in their faith?

What childhood or adult situations brought them to the faith they have now?

4. Consider the choices the children of group members will be making in the future:

What fears do members have?

What hopes do members have?

Are there any guarantees, if so what are they?

Footnotes
[1] *A lion in the meadow*, Margaret Mahy, Picture Puffins.
[2] *Please understand me*, David Keirsey and Marilyn Bates, Prometheus Nemesis Book Company, 1984.

4. TODAY'S PARENTS

During the last two generations styles of parenting and ways of understanding parenting have changed. For a decade there was increased emphasis on mothers dropping their jobs and 'going back' to looking after the home full-time. Subsequently there was considerable interest in giving children a new start and a great reaction against the authoritarian and social class orientation of previous generations. But changes, whether for good or bad, do not happen easily.

VALUES

One aim of parenthood is to raise children to live as responsible adults in society. Childhood might be seen as a preparation for adult life. The child's body grows and matures physically toward adulthood, as long as she has a fairly reasonable physical environment: food, clothing, shelter, warmth and protection from danger. Raising a child to being adult in relationships, in personal responsibility and being able to be a responsible citizen, is parallel to physical growth. There are many aspects which, like food and warmth, help children grow to maturity. Just as a child that doesn't get adequate food suffers from malnutrition and related illnesses, so the child who misses out on the experiences that build maturity, socially does not grow in those areas. The result is immature or 'childish' behaviour in the adult.

However, childhood is not only about what a child will become, but is a state of being, of enjoying life now. A child is more than just an adult in training. In fact, if a child is to become a caring and responsible adult who looks to the good of others as well as herself she should have found during her childhood that it's good to be alive and have been excited about the possibilities of the future because the present is good. The future state, adulthood, is not better than this present state of childhood. There is a natural growth process from feeling good herself to wanting those she loves to feel good and then wanting good even for those people she does not know. It is when a maturing person does not move from the childhood sense of being 'okay' herself, to caring that others are okay, that being a child becomes a social problem.

Thus as we consider our children's daily lives we look for principles that help them find the kinds of experience and relationships that make life good in the present and prepare them for adult life.

Every child is different and every family is different. Sometimes children need to be held back because their adventurousness leads them into danger while others need constant reassurance to get them going. Some families tend to fill their lives with new experiences that encourage children to be adventurous and outward looking. Others find it helpful to look for more ways to get out and about. Some families already have family celebrations and mealtimes that help the whole family enjoy themselves. Others may want to reassess whether TV meals most of the time really are achieving what they want for the family. Every family has good strong points and every family has places where something new could be a valuable addition to its life.

From the time of conception a child is dependent on parents for everything. When she is born she arrives in a family life that is established by her parents, totally dependent on them for care, for love and for growth. Later, others in playgroup and in school contribute to their nurture. But throughout growing life parents have a key role. Even if a child goes away to school most of her perspectives on life are established by the parents.

There are many ways in which society controls family life, strands that control for good and bad. Few families can decide how much money they will have, though to a certain extent they decide how to spend it. Most people have to accept the market rate for their work skills, pay the local rate for rent, and have to own a car where there are no bus services. Every family is irretrievably linked to the local situation. The family can help the child to live happily in her environment, working to change what is bad and can be changed, working around and in spite of what cannot be changed. What is good can be appreciated and enjoyed.

A child grows towards being more involved in society and less dependent on her family. The local community is where a child learns and practises social skills, where she finds a job and looks for leisure activities. Consequently the local area grows to be almost as important as the family in raising children.

It is recognition of the importance of local community life for their families and future generations that causes many people to become involved in working in the local community, taking responsibility on local councils, becoming school governors, helping voluntary organisations that care for neighbours, joining action groups. Some parents in cities have joined groups to fight the increased availability of illegal drugs. Others have formed action groups to campaign for better play facilities, to clean up neighbourhood rubbish and to improve education facilities.

More people than ever before would consider finding the appropriate authority if there are problems locally that cannot be dealt with by individuals or local groups. Many now realise they have access to Members of Parliament, or Boards of Appeal and find ways to have a say in the decisions that affect their lives. Not only does this kind of action help create the kind of environment in which parents want to raise their children but it also teaches the new generation by example how to be among those who influence the quality of life, rather than simply being subject to other people's opinions and policies.

Finding ways to change and influence and even create the kind of society and neighbourhood they want requires of individuals that they learn to work with others. Even when an action group forms for a very specific common purpose (like having something done about a playing field) the members very soon have to come to terms with one another's imperfections. In a family members find ways to get along with one another. So in neighbourhood groups it is soon found that working with others requires acceptance of one another's differences, learning to be more tolerant. People who are unaccepting of human imperfections, (everyone has ways that irritate others sometimes) find themselves living in an isolated and apparently unsympathetic environment. People who can give as well as take, who can laugh at their own shortcomings as well as those of others, who learn how to make the best of a bad job, who face problems with a positive attitude, are more likely to be living a life of openness, with varied and exciting relationships. The children of such parents learn from and eventually become part of their growing relationships, gaining understanding and tolerance.

What values are children learning from those around them?
A teenager from a very troubled area of Belfast, said to me, 'Life's not going to treat you good, life is hard. But you have to face life and get the problems sorted out, just let life go on.'

Experience had taught this young woman at least two major values in life. Life is hard. She had learned this through her experiences on the streets, where rioting and shooting regularly interrupt ordinary daily life.

The other value, 'face life and get the problems sorted out' was learned through close relationships in the family. It is the sort of value that rubs off on children from their parents. With exactly the same social contact, living on the same streets, seeing the same events, other children are despairing. Similarly some people are bitter, others are not; some are forgiving, others never are.

Take a piece of paper and fold it down the middle to make two columns. In one column make a list of all the categories below. Next to each write how this encourages you to believe life is good. For example:

job – suits me
school or playgroup – I get on alright/well with them
relatives – really quite helpful
friends – I could turn to someone in a crisis
neighbours – no real problems
money – not superb but we do alright
marriage – we seem to be learning to sort out the difficulties
children – some problems but we are on the whole okay

Now in the other column write how the same things suggest to you that life is too hard. For example:

job – not good, no prospect for change
schools and playgroup – poor, lack of good facilities
relatives – can't stand any of them
friends – we don't have any that I'd call really good friends
neighbours – they're not very considerate
money – it's an uphill struggle all the time
marriage – we have nothing but problems
children – I don't know what I'm doing wrong, but . . . we seem to have endless problems

At the bottom of the page beneath the two columns draw some scales, like this:

---

good   bad and put an X in the scale pan you think is heaviest. Not necessarily because it has the most items on the list but on the whole you think more that life is good or life is bad.

Making a list like the one above, all of us tend to put the X in the scale pan that corresponds to our predominant approach to life. If we were to repeat the exercise every day for a while then every one of us would make changes to the weighting. But those who basically believe life to be good would on the bad days find themselves looking for a solution to the problem, while those who mostly see life as bad find a new insurmountable problem if yesterday's has now gone away.

In Christian terms we have a sense of hope or of doom that colours our views. We may see problems around us but look confidently towards finding solutions to them, knowing the hope we have in Christ. Alternatively we may see the problems and struggle not to be overwhelmed, fearful and unsure of any redemption of our particular concerns. These are deeply held attitudes, often we bring the positive or negative approach to life into our Christian discipleship with us. A balanced faith will lead us to recognise that it is not our life attitude, positive or negative, that determines the nature of the reality of our everyday life but the goodness of God. Our attitude colours how we see his goodness.

It's as if everyone has two possible pairs of spectacles through which to look at life, a hopeful one or a despairing one. One lens shows 'Now, how can I tackle this problem?' while the other shows 'It's too much. That's the last straw.' Such perspectives come from the person's basic personality and experience of life. This may not be the time to consider whether these can be changed, but it is very helpful to be able to see which lens we use most of the time and when we use which, then we know what life values we are communicating to our children.

It may be helpful to you to talk with your marriage partner about the spectacles each of you use most of the time at home, as you may then be able to draw on your particular strengths. If you tend to be pessimistic when the family faces a problem together you may wish to make sure that your partner's view is clearly heard; they may have a positive attitude to problem solving. Spectacles are not such a problem when we recognise them for what they are rather than just looking through them unawares.

Values and attitudes are expressed in the daily routines and activities of the family, and children learn from these. Relationship values are evident in the parents' relationship and speak far louder than words.

Openness: do members of your family say what they think or are there hidden controls? Is there freedom to say what they think or are only certain kinds of thoughts and feelings freely expressed?

No-go areas: married couples have topics they don't talk about. He knows she's 'touchy' on a certain subject. She has realised he'll withdraw if she raises certain others. Some couples are unable to talk about money, others about sex, others about illness, others about particular relatives or friendships. The children sense that certain subjects are taboo, without knowing why.

In your family, do you *really* listen to each other, not just nod and carry on as if the other person's thoughts and feelings are less important or less right? Do the adults in the family sulk when things don't go as they wish? Do they manipulate one another or circumstances to get their own way, rather than being direct? What are the unspoken values, judgements and actions that you are teaching your children – not just occasionally but day in, day out?

The importance in reflecting on these values in family life is that these hidden messages teach the children values. If one of the parents is constantly over-ridden by the other, the children very soon do exactly the same, disregarding that same parent and avoiding his discipline. If your child seems to repeat a particular attitude that you consider 'bad' or 'negative' look at yourselves – you may be teaching her to do it.

One family talked to me about their children's table manners. There seemed to be a constant problem and although the children were no longer small they had to be endlessly reminded on certain points. A meal with the family immediately revealed a major contribution to the problem. Mum was very neat at the table while Dad was the opposite, chewing with his mouth open, talking while he had his mouth full and resting his elbows on the table. The parents were trying to get the children to behave as the mother behaved. So the two children while being told constantly not to do these things were experiencing another model. If the parents were going to succeed in what they were wanting to do they were going to have to change Dad's way of eating as well as the children's.

CONFLICTING VALUES

'Peter's mum gave us tea in front of the telly, Mum. Why won't you let us have tea in front of the telly at home?' All parents have probably heard some version of that complaint, voiced in any form from a minor question to a full-scale tantrum. What can be done when our children find that there are different values being presented in different places?

Children very soon discover the difference between their parents. For some things they go to Dad, while for others they go to Mum. If Mum has said 'No' they may try to persuade Dad to give them permission, or want him to become an ally. Such 'deviousness' may reflect simply that Mum and Dad value certain things differently. Dad may think it's very important for the family to sit at the table together for meals, while Mum enjoys a meal together but is really not too fussed either way.

Does this matter? Is it really important? Some children are distressed by such differences and continue to ask questions that point out the two conflicting opinions. To be unsure which answer they may receive makes them insecure. Other children are happy living with the difference; they'll work within one limit while with Dad and quite happily change to another an hour later with Mum. Some parents are happy with different values. For others, the result is a major conflict within the family. Usually the higher the value is on the list of a parent's priorities the more they are affronted if this is not valued equally by their partner. Perhaps the rule was so drummed into them while *they* were growing up that all they can do is be equally insistent with their own children. If the difference in values causes problems in the family then it's worth taking time to talk about the situation.

Consider the following examples which show some expectations parents have, where commonly there are varying views. Each example shows two extremes. On the line between the two, put an x to show how important this question is to you. For example, if please and thank you are very important put an x near to the right end of the line.

'It is good to be friendly and polite, but I don't mind much if they forget please and thank you'   'Please and thank you are among the most important things to learn'

'Some fighting is normal between children'   'I don't ever allow children to fight'

'I want my children to look neat and presentable'   'Scruffy kids are happy kids'

Having put in an x that reflects your values on these issues, draw in an arrow where you think your spouse would come on the line.

The further apart the two marks are, the more likely it is that there is conflict between you.

To resolve the conflict of very different values it is necessary to understand why you believe in these so strongly. Write down two or three of your own examples, habits which irritate you intensely when children do them or behaviour that irritates you intensely when other people 'let children get away with it'.

Remember how you were taught about such values as a child? Were you nagged, spanked, threatened, told you were hopeless? How did your parents insist on these values for you? Are these values that you have accumulated unconsciously?

Very few of the values we worry about are matters of life and death. Even if we find children fighting it may be that they simply need help to find a peaceful solution. More often we would be less anxious about such principles if we could talk over what has happened to us, what we fear and how much we really want to insist on the values with which we were raised.

An open conversation on the subject, looking at how each of you came to your present position, can help pave the way to a common expectation for the future.

Many parents are worried about what they are teaching their children about life values, whether they are too strict or too lax, or totally missing the point. The above method helps them talk together about their value judgements, helps in avoiding extremes, and in a responsible way helps them to change with the times and generations. Talk to other parents about this subject, letting them place their x's on the line as an opener.

List any other values that you hold differently from your spouse. Find time to talk about them together, till you appreciate one another's viewpoint.

QUESTIONS FOR INDIVIDUALS AND GROUPS

1. In discovering your own attitude to life, positive or negative, would you say you are sometimes one and sometimes the other? What determines your attitude, what discourages you?

Do you see your family affected by the way you feel about life? How?

Note any changes you would like to make if you could.

2. Are there biblical principles that teach us about life attitudes, and God's goodness?

Consider the following passages: do they relate to attitudes and values?

Matthew 6:25–34
Matthew 11:28–30
Romans 8:28–39
Psalm 23
Psalm 46

QUESTIONS FOR GROUPS

1. Hear from members of the group about their attitudes to life. What did they discover in the Scriptures given?
2. Consider as a group the places at which you find conflicting values in families.

As a group list the values that are important to you and your families.

As a group list those values for family life that you believe are essentially Christian. Discuss these to see if the whole group agrees on them. Probably you will find there are a few which every member will wholeheartedly endorse as Christian and lots over which you have various shades of opinion, depending on your backgrounds. Then discuss also whether these values are directly Scriptural or how they relate to biblical injunctions.

As Christians what values do you wish to give your children that are not upheld by society around you? Make a list, referring to the list above. How can you help your children to respect these Christian values?

5. PARENTING ROLES

Traditions help instil an image of father and mother in a family, with regard to the ways that parents act out roles in relation to their children's upbringing.

Next to each of the responsibilities listed below write whether you would generally expect a mother or a father to fulfil this role.

Now think of yourself and your partner as parents. In another colour write next to each category the way you now fulfil these roles. For example, mother as well as father may be wage-earners. Both may concern themselves about children's schooling.

Responsibilities   *expectations*   *how we do these*

wage-earner

diet and nutrition

children's bedtimes

buying children's clothes

preparing meals

discipline

education

visiting teachers/parents evening

comfort and affection

help with school work

food buying

meal preparation

outings

While many of today's parents grew up with a strong traditional pattern of parenting roles in which fathers were the disciplinarians and mothers those who cared and nurtured, many of these have had to change. Today the majority of mothers have work outside the home at least part-time.

Bringing up children has become a job in which both parents share the necessary work, as well as the enjoyment, of the nurturing relationship with their child. This is a healthy pattern for the child, who benefits greatly from having a significant close relationship with both parents. Each parent is a model for the child's attitudes, behaviour and communication patterns. For effective upbringing, both parents should be giving time and active involvement to the child, with love and affection.

MOTHERS

Women have been the primary 'carers' during a child's infant years, resulting in a firm impression that only women can do this work, that it is part of their nature and not that of men. Obviously, girls have learned about the role from watching and identifying with their own mothers, and boys learned other roles. But the role can be fulfilled effectively by father: he can change nappies, keep schedules for feeding and sleeping, do laundry, play, take walks, be affectionate and intimate and generally act as 'mother'.

In some families, the list above has been a complete reversal of the traditional patterns, as parents fill in their own pattern.

Lone fathers cope well with the tasks of childcare and housework, as do husbands whose wife is handicapped. It is well known that John Lennon took care of home and baby until his son Sean was five, while Yoko Ono took care of business and finance.

One result of traditional roles is that men's wages are higher than women's. So in most families the cost of living requires that father work full-time. Deciding on a complete reversal of the traditional roles is, for this reason, unusual. But it is helpful, however, to realise that if mother also has a job outside the home to help the family's income, some of the work usually associated with being housewife is taken up by father. Unfortunately, research has shown that where woman and man both work outside the home, the woman still does most of the childcare and housework.

Nurture, support and encouragement have tended to be mother's work. The child's developmental needs including starting playgroup and getting ready for school are left to mother. Children whose parents both take a full interest in their schooling and general growth tend to be above average in their progress. Both Mum and Dad can encourage and help with homework, listen to reading or spelling, or help with maths.

If as a family you decide to fulfil the parenting roles in a way different from your childhood experience, decide not only who will take up the responsibility but how is that parent going to learn what is involved. In a previous chapter there was recognition that most adults parent the way they were brought up, or in reaction to those patterns. So if father is going to be concerned in some of the roles traditionally belonging to mother, he may need to learn more, reading about babies, their development, their schedules; finding out about visiting the clinic and the regular medical check-up that is given; discovering the symptoms of childhood ailments. Mothering also includes a relatively intangible quality of affection, attention, loyalty, and self-sacrifice, that is not related so much to a particular task as to the way that task is done.

Self-sacrifice is a deep-seated tradition among women. It's an extremely important aspect of mothering, yet one that could be shared equally by both parents. Caring agencies in various countries have discovered that women expect to sacrifice their own interests for the sake of their family, while men expect this of themselves less often. In giving aid in the form of money, some agencies discovered that a woman receiving aid more often spent the money on a useful commodity such as a goat for the family. If the man of the family received it, he was more likely to spend the money on a transistor radio to improve his own status. Hence, the agencies are attempting to ensure that money gets into the hands of mothers, for the best possible help to the family.

Discipline should not be left to one parent. Nor should a punishment be held over 'till your Dad gets in from work'. To make Dad the disciplinarian, or to use him as a threat breaks down the child's relationship with her father. If mother has reason to correct a child's behaviour, then this should be followed through at the time.

While making the shopping list, encourage children, boys as well as girls, to help and in so doing learn the process of decision-making. After a meal ask the boys to wash up as often as the girls. Both boys and girls should learn cooking, ironing and cleaning. Through their working with you, both boys and girls can learn how and when to do chores, such as cooking and cleaning.

Most young adults spend some time living alone or will later have sole responsibility for children. Through your expectations and sharing the work with them they will be more able to cope when they in turn reach adulthood. Boys who have not learned such skills as children have to use more time and energy to do even simple 'housewifely' tasks, like mending clothes, than girls who have both expected to do it and learned how to as they grew.

Mothers tend to talk about the problems of motherhood when they get together. This is not surprising, really, as they spend so much of their time trying to hold the many aspects in balance. Housekeeping money, clothing costs, child's growth rate, what's normal and what is abnormal: all these are common concerns, common worries, and so are better shared. The more both parents share the concerns, the less insular mother feels in her interests. The nature of mothering and the amount of responsibility involved means that mothers always want to talk about these responsibilities and how to handle them better.

FATHERS

There has been very little significant research into the meaning and effectiveness of fathering. This has perhaps been affected by the lack of examples, as the traditional role for fathers gave men a relatively minor active role in their child's life. Up until this century in Britain, ownership of children was considered exclusively the father's right, as could be seen from the expectations of custody in marriage breakdown. However, today in cases of marriage breakdown, custody far more often goes with the mother who is seen to be the more significant adult in the children's lives. At the level of daily living, since mothers have provided more of the emotional stability, the daily nurturing, and the oversight of developmental needs, one result has been an apparent absence of meaning for fathers. With the realisation that ownership is an invalid state between people, even of children, the nature of fathering should be, but has not yet been, redefined.

If fathers are going to have a significant active role in their children's lives, in their development and approach to life, they must join in reassessing their own approach to the roles listed at the beginning of the chapter. Fathering *can* mean what parents want fathering to mean. Most of the parenting roles may be shared, except for the physical process of pregnancy and birth. But from that moment on, a father can be as involved and as responsible as a mother, and most mothers would be glad to share the responsibility more fully. Parenting is a joint and equal venture and each couple should decide how they are going to fulfil the roles. The best father to have is the one who is totally involved in his child's life.

There are qualities that a significant father-figure communicates to a child in the early years. Just as a mother expresses femininity, a father models masculinity. The absence of a significant male relationship can leave young boys unsure of themselves and their identity. The relationship between parents, as a man and a woman, and the different ways in which they tackle daily life, enables the child to become secure in his or her own identity and sexuality.

Children whose fathers are interested in their schooling are more likely to learn steadily and consistently or even to be above average. Whether this is specifically because having two parents interested results in twice the affirmation or that there is a quality of interest offered particularly by fathers, is not known.

The father's expressions of affection and involvement in play and games with the child help build self-esteem. The interest of a different person with another creative approach to what they do, reaffirms the child's sense that they are a worthwhile and likeable person.

Father's choice to spend time with his child on outings that interest them together, or taking up hobbies they can tackle together, results in the child having greater curiosity and interest in what's going on around. A boy whose father is actively interested and spends time with him is less likely to be bored and aimless.

A man's earning potential is usually greater than his wife's, so it may go without question that he should be the family's chief wage-earner. Within the next few years women's wages will probably be equivalent to those of men; and many areas of high unemployment have more jobs for women than for men. But the power in the family should still be divided between the parents and there should be no assumption of priority of position as a result of performing this particular role. The *role* of wage-earner is not a sign of superiority or relative importance. The division of roles in parenting must not be accompanied by judgements on status, for this destroys a healthy environment for growing children. If the male sense of identity is based on a false superiority related to earnings, men will suffer a considerable identity crisis in the family and society and feel emasculated when the wife is able to earn more money.

Many fathers are distanced from the life of the children by pressures at work. The drive to succeed and to earn more may, in certain types of work, take them away from home more and more. The loss of time and attention is often a far greater loss than is justified by increased wages. Many fathers suddenly realise in middle age that their children are virtual strangers and the close relationship they would have wanted with them is now permanently lost. Achieving ambitions is only part of any person's source of fulfilment in life. Deep, satisfying relationships are of equal or greater significance in the long run.

On the occasions that I have asked fathers how much time they have spent thinking and talking with others about what it means to be a father, or how much they have talked to other fathers about the hows and whys of parenting, I have received a singular response. None. In itself, this is a reflection of the fact that most of the parenting work has been done by women, that fathers are relatively unaffirmed in their responsibilities, and that many people do not realise how helpful it is to talk together. Fathers would be helped a great deal in relating to their children if they could also find the close and affirming friendships that mothers find, where conversation can include topics related to their various offspring. Joint reflection is a key way to coping with changes in parenting. Fathers would benefit greatly if they could talk more.

Essentially, fathering is defined by the ways in which men get involved actively in parenting. While the roles of women have changed considerably in contemporary society, men too have to cope with a change to shared power, shared concern and new attitudes to money, assets and ownership. All these have negated previous status-oriented approaches to fathering and provide an opening for fathers to choose an active, supporting, and encouraging role in their children's lives, an opportunity for shared parenting.

WORKING MOTHERS — WHERE BOTH PARENTS WORK OUTSIDE THE HOME

For many families, it is a financial necessity for both parents to work outside the home. The effect of this situation on a child varies with age and circumstances.

A baby or toddler very much needs an environment that is stimulating, while very stable, with secure relationships. The close relationship with the parent who is at home usually provides these aspects. But if mother as well as father go out to work, will alternative childcare be able to meet these needs? Whether parents look to a relative or to a child minder, that person must genuinely enjoy children's company, and the company of their child in particular; this must not be 'just a job'. The new adult must have time to get to know the child as well as if she were The minder's own child, having time to enjoy the baby's company, to enjoy playing with her and readily show her affection. The stimulation for language and social development comes from interchanges with the adult who cares for her. A baby or toddler can cope with several significant adults in her life, but not too many; there must be consistent minding with the same person.

Even with the best child-care, interaction with parents is vital to a baby or toddler. Despite the pressure of chores and housework, ensure that parents spend plenty of undivided time with the baby in the evenings and on weekends.

Once a child is three to four years old there is positive benefit in her getting away from home for a few hours each week. This can be compatible with mother's part-time work. Playgroups and nursery schools give a child a sense of independence and more opportunity to play with other children. Having been at

Parenting Roles

playgroup while mother is at work, the child has lots more stimulation for conversation when she is home again.

Infant or First school children may at first find it hard to be away from home so long. The bigger world of school can seem insecure if a child is aware that mother is not at home either. Explain fully to your child where you are working, when you will be home, and what she can expect when she gets home. Make sure she knows that the school staff know how to contact you if she becomes sick and who will look after her if she has to stay at home.

As she gets older and accustomed to mother's work, a child is quite happy about the situation. If possible, find an occasion when a child can visit the parent's work place so she can imagine fairly accurately what mum is doing.

Older children and teenagers positively benefit from working mothers. The concept of mother having a life of her own, rather than being everyone's back-up person, is helpful, and the social contact and interest she finds in people and work adds to the quality of life at home.

Having two working parents does have the disadvantage that all the work of running a family home falls on the evenings and weekends. Since both parents are out during the day, it is reasonable to expect both mother and father to share the work when they are home. They may be tempted to concentrate only on getting chores done. For a child's education, however, make sure one parent is spending time with the child, on education-related tasks – such as stories, reading, playing family games, or just talking. Parents should resist the temptation to leave the child in front of the television while they get on with the chores.

Many of the tasks that make up family life like shopping at the supermarket, might be quicker and easier without a child's company, but remember a child learns by being with parents. In any case, the older children of working mothers are often happy to lend a hand by doing the shopping if they are familiar with how it's done.

The children of working mums often have more responsibility and have more social skills. As a result they are more mature and able to fend for themselves, and less accustomed to having someone available to do things for them.

QUESTIONS FOR INDIVIDUALS AND GROUPS

1. Fill in the chart from the beginning of the chapter if you have not already done so.
2. What is a father? Write notes on your own experience as a child.
   What do you think now that fathering should mean?
3. If in your family both you and your partner work outside the home, go over the role functions and look at how you fulfil those. Discuss its effectiveness with your partner.

QUESTIONS FOR GROUPS

1. Using a large sheet of paper on the wall, collect and write up the ways in which the group is fulfilling the roles of parenting.
2. Discuss parenting roles, which tasks should or could be shared or done by either parent specifically?
   Read together Proverbs 31:10–31. As the writer of Proverbs brought together all the ideals of his culture to describe the ideal woman, how would this description fit in our society today? Which of the tasks are normally now expected of women? For example, the muscle building of verse 17 would be considered not very feminine today. Which of the tasks would we expect of both father and mother in the family? This passage considers attitudes, work, relationships, diligence, beauty, generosity. Putting together such aspects, as a group make a description more appropriate for today.
3. Using another large sheet of paper, write up members' suggestions for what it means to be a father.
4. When you have a parents' meeting or discussion in your church, do mothers and fathers attend equally? Why is the balance what it is?
   Do parents, fathers and mothers, have or take equal chance to learn about parenting?
5. Looking at biblical references to parenting, discover the passages that the group considers most relevant to their situations.

6. LEARNING AND GROWING

During the first five years a child learns more than at any other stage of her life, forming a foundation for attitudes to life and learning that are to come as she gets older. While at home before starting school, a small child has more undivided attention than she will ever get again. Even though mother has work to do, she gives considerable time and attention to her child. Subsequently, instead of having the undivided attention of a parent for significant blocks of time, the child who starts school has to share the teacher's attention with up to thirty-five other children. Even in playgroup the odds are never as good as at home.

Parents have the opportunity to provide their child with a good foundation for life skills and for formal education. The scope is endless without ever tackling tasks, such as reading, which may be best left to the teacher. In the cosier atmosphere at home, the parent's interest and affirming responses can encourage the child's curiosity, open the way for interest in learning and affirm individual creativity and expression.

The world is a fascinating and exciting place. Adults take many things for granted, or may be too busy to appreciate them any more. Having a small child with you is a good opportunity to reflect on what's around you, her fresh approach seeing things with new eyes. If your child is fascinated by a creature, someone working, or an unusual object when you are out walking, stop and watch for a while; let her appreciate and wonder about it. Listen and watch: there is no need for you to comment though you may get involved in conversation that introduces your child to new words.

As you see nature and creation around you, treat it with reverence and respect and your child will too. Whether you live in the town or country, there are birds all around. Make a bird table or use the window ledge to feed them, get to know their names. Watch as they collect nesting materials, fly, hop or hover. Look out for their nests, around the house and in the gardens and parks. Listen for the cuckoo or the sound of pigeons on the roof.

Dogs and cats are everywhere. Unfamiliar animals may not be friendly, and even well known ones should be patted with care. Visit zoos and farms, where there are animals to look at and appreciate. It's only when a child meets them in real life that she realises their size and that they are alive. On the page of a book they are static shapes and could be stuffed toys. If you take a small child to see animals at the zoo she may not be able to concentrate long or maintain interest, so avoid trying to see everything in one visit.

There are trees and greenery in all sorts of places. Even wild flowers grow between paving stones or on high walls and gutters. If there's a chance, let your child climb trees and visit woodland and forests. The ground is different in woodland than in parks and fields and is covered with many small plants, fallen leaves and tree stumps.

Turn over stones and see what's underneath. A child may initially be afraid of insects, but familiarity helps. If she doesn't want to touch them, don't make her. Point out insects that sting, as well as spiders in their webs.

Look up at the sky. See the shapes of the clouds and their colours. Feel the rain and snow as they fall. Walk though puddles. The wind blows rubbish and leaves along the street and, in the open country, trees are blown wildly.

Consider the awareness of creation shown by the biblical poetry in the Psalms and in passages such as Isaiah 55:10–13. The Proverbs have an interesting study of ants and the busy way that they go about their work. A fresh look engendered through the curiosity of our children can bring a renewed sense of God in creation.

A child's senses are very alert, taking in all her new experiences. A child enjoys different shapes and textures as she holds and plays with them. Many commercial toys are plastic and smooth, find other things to play with. Pick up sand, wood, and stone. Put natural objects among the toddler's collection of toys. Let her play in the bath, feel the water and enjoy it.

Colour is a stimulating aspect in a child's world, so have lots of it. Make sure her clothes are variously coloured, and while you may have a favourite, let your child try them all. Remember, the idea that colours clash is an adult fashion concept. Babies don't particularly like pastel shades and white; when they wave their hands and feet around it's much more

Learning and Growing

fun to see bright and attractive colours. Look out for striped baby clothes.

Hang a brightly coloured mobile over the baby's bed and put pictures on the wall where they can be seen. Furniture and bedclothes can be bright; a baby spends quite a lot of time awake in bed before it is time to get up.

Many sounds are new and fascinating. Close your eyes for a moment and list the sounds you can hear. They are so familiar that we hardly hear them, though if all our surroundings are suddenly silent we may be worried. A child will remain frightened of loud sounds if their source is unknown. She may like to find the source of some sounds, to satisfy her curiosity.

Sounds have an important history among God's people. Music has been a vehicle for worshipping God throughout history, and in a variety of forms. Look again at Psalm 150 for a description of a noisy time of praise. As Joshua led the people of Israel in walking around Jericho, the people were instructed to make no sound, but the priests blew trumpets continually. Only on the seventh day did the people shout, so loudly that the walls fell. Shouting can be useful as well as fun.

Taste and smell are much more sensitive in a child than in an adult. For this reason a child may refuse certain foods, but parents should keep offering them, the day will come when they will enjoy them. There are smells in the house, of cooking or of soap in the bath. There are smells on the street of smoke or fumes. Fruits smell in the greengrocers. When you notice a particular smell, point it out and name it for your child.

When preparing food for children, find a variety of tastes, savoury and sweet, salty and sugary. Use raw vegetables as well as cooked ones. Don't always take the skins off the apples and tomatoes and serve foods that need chewing as well as the smooth textures.

A child has many feelings, just as an adult does. In a child they are less controlled and more likely to overflow in an emotional outburst, either tears, tantrums, or shouts of joy. As parents shares their feeling with their child, the child can learn and begin to name her own feelings. This is a vital step in emotional and social maturity. The person who knows his own reactions and responses is far more likely to be able to choose how to express them, and to establish communication with friends more effectively.

Bodies are very important to the baby and toddler. They are not only discovering what they can do, but what they are. Help a small child appreciate and name the parts of her body.

Explain gender without being prudish. Accept sexuality as a normal and beautiful part of his life. Some parts of the body may be kept private and the child can be encouraged to keep exploration of genitals for private times; don't be tempted to call them rude or dirty, or even imply it. By your respect let your child know you like and enjoy your body and she can enjoy hers.

In Psalm 139 the psalmist reflects on the care of God in creating a person, while the child was being formed in the mother's womb. There are parts of a person that are hidden, but not from God who made the whole body. The body is covered but not unacceptable.

Society is full of images that are considered beautiful or better as far as bodies are concerned. Certain female bodies, currently the thinner ones, and certain male bodies, usually the muscular ones, are upheld as patterns of beauty. That can be condemning to those whose bodies are more run-of-the-mill and whose faces are more like those seen every day on the street. Most people who enjoy life, who enjoy themselves and are self-accepting, are attractive and acceptable to their friends too. Don't make your child feel bad about herself. Enjoy her as she is and then she will enjoy being herself. When children reach their teens and become interested in new and 'outrageous' fashions, enjoy *them* for what they are – a new generation's enjoyment and celebration of their life and looks. Don't be critical.

Listen, and enjoy your child's stories and songs as she makes them up. Fantasy and imagination in a small child are relatively unhampered by the necessity of realism or preconceived ideas.

Learning and Growing 65

OPPORTUNITIES FOR GROWTH

No-one can make a child grow, learn, or discover. She learns for herself. However, if the environment is rich, full of opportunity, new experiences, and challenges, the child's own inner drive is multiplied and developed. Curiosity is stimulated by new people, places and things. There is time to explore, test and experiment, time to wonder and relax.

From the earliest possible moment talk to and with your baby. While she may only respond with smiles or unformed sounds, she understands your tone and your meaning long before she has learned to communicate and form words for herself. Stories and conversation, rhymes and songs feed language skills and give the child time and opportunity to practice. The foundational shapes of language and communication are formed in very young children; as they grow they learn more vocabulary and finer aspects of language. Early play with words and stories and ideas enables the child to communicate and understand, to think and deliberate. Negotiation with other people, the route to the resolution of conflict and the possibility of compromise, is based on this early language development.

Play

Play takes many forms and has a multitude of purposes. Play is self-motivated activity, done for its own sake. Children play to satisfy themselves, to challenge themselves, to do things they have never done before. They try to find answers to their own questions. There is a seemingly endless drive to play.

What sorts of opportunity for play should parents provide for a child?

There is play for self-expression and self-realisation as well as play that mimics adult behaviour and practises life-skills. Look at the following suggestions and see if there is something new you could introduce for your child.

A child tries out the things she can do with her own body, crawling on the floor, on grass, on sand, and on stones. A baby begins to pull herself up to standing, with the rails of the cot, against chairs and other furniture. Once on their feet they walk and run, try to go backwards, and one day they are hopping and skipping. Take your child on walks in all sorts of countryside as well as the town, on rough ground, over hills, through long grass and scrub. Walk on the beach where the sand slips away and makes hard work of moving. A small child may get tired sooner than you: a piggy-back ride can be fun for her; she will enjoy being close to you and seeing the world from a height. Before starting school they enjoy learning to pedal a tricycle or push a doll's pram. Steering, at first a puzzle, is soon mastered.

There are many children's toys that are for building and all forms of construction, some very sophisticated. Odd blocks of wood from the home workshop can be used for building and the kitchen has many utensils that can be stacked and fitted together. Building and fitting help a child's basic understanding of quantity and spatial concepts; these are necessary foundations to mathematical development.

Teach your child to use scissors and kitchen tools. Use scaled down carpentry tools that really work but won't cause too much damage to fingers or to furniture. By using tools and utensils alongside parents, a child learns not only how but also when to use various tools. Provide an apron, a rolling pin and some pastry when you cook and later let them weigh, measure and mix the ingredients themselves.

Introduce your child to water. Take her to the swimming pool; there are parent and toddler lessons at lots of public swimming pools. Washing-up becomes a favourite though long-winded pastime as it involves lots of pouring and passing to-and-fro. Let the child play with empty plastic containers and wash items like unbreakable baking tins, allowing lots of time. Encourage her to keep the water in the sink but resign yourself to the fact that some spillage is inevitable. A child may help you mop it up, quite gladly. Learning to pour accurately is preceded by pouring inaccurately; better to learn over the sink than over the carpet. As soon as possible, let your child pour her own drinks, spoon food onto a plate, pass things to others and serve them. Limit the child's participation when there is danger involved but as far as possible let them try everything.

From the age of three or four upwards children enjoy play that re-enacts the life and work of people around them and the experiences of ordinary life. Dolls and teddies become babies, disciplined, fed, and put to bed. Children themselves become mother and father, doctor, nurse, dentist, teacher, minister and any other roles they meet day by day. The children rehearse the activities they have seen with an accuracy that often shows remarkable perception as well as showing their personal response to what happened. Such play is best aided by a dressing-up box of clothes from jumble sales; include coats, hats, dresses, trousers and shirts. Often at jumble sales the bric-a-brac table yields miscellaneous jewellery, buttons and beads, and can also be a source of pots and pans for play, for just a

Learning and Growing

few pence. The children often do this shopping for themselves, so adding to the value of the experience.

NEW PEOPLE

New people are exciting and interesting. Introduce a small child especially to people who are interested in her, though don't attempt to force the child to be friendly. Let them take their own time, just as an adult does with new faces. A baby can enjoy close relationships with several people in the family, or close circle of acquaintances.

Introduce the child to the baby sitter and let them become acquainted before you leave the baby sitter in charge. Your child might well be very upset, and justifiably so, if she wakes up to find a complete stranger there, especially when she wakes distressed or uncomfortable.

Find opportunity for other adults to take charge of your child and for her to belong to a group of children. For example, both Sunday School and Playgroup provide friendly environments that can be a bridge to coping with the new people they will meet in school when they are five.

Just as talking and playing with parents gives opportunity for learning communication skills, play with other children gives opportunity to negotiate as equals, to learn to overcome misunderstandings, to invent games and play as peers. Giving your child opportunity to meet other children is, therefore, a special need if you have only one child. Without the opportunity of play with sisters and brothers she may otherwise have little opportunity to establish friendships with children of her own age.

There are many other people your child sees around the home and meets during the course of the day. The milkman, the postman, the coalman, the chimney sweep – all have work to do that fascinates a child and stirs her imagination. Find books that illustrate the work of these people.

Shopkeepers are regular contacts. Through shopping with parents a child understands the routines of shopping, how and why to pay for goods. There are many kinds of shops and if a parent is going to the garden centre or the DIY superstore take the child along so they can see what happens there.

Explain to your child what nurses, doctors, and dentists do, and how they treat her. Sometimes treatment is painful; if it's going to hurt, be truthful and say so. On the whole, guard against making your child afraid of pain, but instead show how

NEW PLACES

A child's curiosity and interest in discovery is fed by new experience and new places. Some may be easily within your reach and some may be so commonplace to you that you overlook your child's potential interest.

Castles and zoos are attractions that can be exciting to visit. Tell your child the history of a castle you want to visit, and how castles were used to protect whole villages of people. Relate the stories of King Arthur and his knights. She may have lots of questions when you reach your castle, 'Where were the animals kept?' and 'Where were the toilets?'

Visit rivers, for fishing or travelling on a boat. Walk along the bank and if you can visit a canal, watch the lock in operation as boats go up and down. A child faced with a stream or brook may begin by paddling, stopping the flow with his feet but eventually progressing to building bridges and dams. A child discovers this herself, given a little opportunity.

Visit museums for several short visits, whetting the appetite and gauging the length of visit from the level of your child's interest and concentration span. Small children, however, may find little of interest except in those museums that specialise in models of real life, or in full-size vehicles, such as those in the Science Museum in London.

Most areas of the country offer the possibility of visiting open countryside or heathland. Climb hills, walk over heathland, pick wild flowers and berries, observing the country code as you do so. If you know a farm you can visit, introduce your child to the animal pens and sheds. See as many types of farm work as you can, from feeding animals to collecting eggs and milking the cows. This may seem rather hard for town dwellers. But look for the particular opportunities that you have to use buses and trains. Visit the places where things are made, where the firemen work, the brewery horses, and the city farms (a new development in small farms in urban areas, giving city children opportunity for contact with farming). There are working canals in urban areas as well as markets where animals are bought and sold. Begin exploring your area with your child; who knows what you may find.

Your holidays may include visiting the sea, which is an exciting experience for small children. At first your child may be afraid of the waves and water – don't hurry her, let her move at her own pace. When a child is very small you'll find it helpful, for your enjoyment of a holiday, to keep the routine as near as possible to the usual schedule at home, or you may have disturbed nights. However, there are some children who are happy with late nights and unusual circumstances – as long as meals are at approximately the normal time.

The discovery of what is new and exciting, stimulates curiosity and sense of adventure. The opportunity to touch, see, taste, and hear creation suggests to a child that the world is a wonderful place full of mystery and treasure worthy of his efforts in searching. The parents' attitudes, of reverence for what is precious, of tenderness with what is fragile, of abhorrence for the repellent, of courage in the face of challenge, are all communicated to the child.

QUESTIONS FOR INDIVIDUAL AND GROUP STUDY

1. Write down the following:
   – a memory of play with other children when you were playing out roles that you had seen adults performing, such as mothers and fathers or hospitals.

   – a family outing, when you specially enjoyed the company of mum or dad and the activity you did together. What was the warm feeling you associate with this time?

   – a place you visited that for you was special, it may have been a high hill or mountain, a stream where you were allowed to paddle, a river, castle or beach.

   Do you have any idea how old you were when these things happened?

2. Reflect on the warmth and goodness of God to you in a variety of ways:
   – in people, those who know and love you. Write down the names of someone you can have a good laugh with, someone to whom you would go if distressed, someone who you think is wise, someone with whom you would tackle a new challenge.

   – in creation, the affirming beauty of what surrounds you. Write down your favourite meal, your favourite relaxation. Write down too what you appreciate about hearing and sight.

   – in life. What is God's most significant gift to you, whether it is an ability he has given you, the people he has placed in your life, or some other aspect of your experience. When did you first realise what a gift this was? Did you thank God for this and do you go on thanking him?

QUESTIONS FOR GROUPS

1. Read together Job 38:3–41:34. God points out to Job the wonders of creation. As a group devise ways that you can introduce your children to wonders such as these.

   Share with one another your own experiences when seeing creation has impressed you with the majesty of God.

2. Listen to one another's reflections on childhood.

3. Consider the children of the group's members and of the church. What opportunities are being provided for them to have new experience of life, people, and activities?

   – Can any of you offer skills to help, eg are you skilled at sailing or swimming, and could teach others? Do any of you

Learning and Growing

go on walks and would like to take a child with you? Do any of you have facilities that you could share with others, eg. a large garden with opportunity for children to play, climb and run around? Perhaps you have space for children to help cook a barbecue meal, or perhaps someone has a swimming pool to which others could have access.

– Would the group like to organise an outing, perhaps a coach party, to somewhere of interest to families, adults and children? (Often it is helpful to find a way for families with more children and for single parents to have a lower per capita charge for an outing as their resources are more stretched.) If this is relevant make plans together.

7. LEARNING FOR LIFE

There are many skills which parents are well qualified to teach their children and many everyday activities that a family can do together to help the foundations of educational skills. Some are life skills and others are helpful learning skills.

LIFE SKILLS

A child may be potty-trained by the time she is two years old or soon after. Before she starts school, help the child cope with cleaning her own bottom, to get beyond calling out 'Mum, I've finished', and expecting someone to come to help. Very occasionally a child at school wets herself because she is unsure of herself or the situation. Make sure she knows how to ask for the toilet when she needs to and how to ask where it is. The child may have had a family word for asking to go to the toilet but now is the time for learning a way that others understand, 'Can I go to the toilet, please?' Teachers understand it is very hard for a small child to wait and many infant classes have toilets adjacent to them. Tell your child to ask before they reach desperation. It is unlikely that a teacher would expect her to wait till playtime.

The school classroom does not have the same staff ratio as playgroup. Some infant classes have a helper for part of the day in addition to the class teacher for the thirty or more children. A child's personal care should include being able to wash her own face and hands, wiping her hands thoroughly and leaving the sink tidy. Changing for games into shorts or even into swimsuits involves being able to dress and change shoes. Help your child with having clothes the right way out, doing up buttons, tying laces and checking whether she has forgotten anything. Schools normally ask parents to sew nametapes into clothing, to help when items are mislaid.

For wintry weather a child should be able to cope with hats, gloves and coat. Teach her to do up the open-ended zips that are on many anoraks. If your child has an anorak or similar coat, remove any strings on the body, hood or neck. These have resulted in fatal accidents with children getting hooked by the string when climbing, hanging themselves in their struggle to get free. Better safe than sorry.

Show your child how to cross the road where the patrol 'lollipop' person is there to help, or where there is a Panda crossing. *Do not allow her to cross anywhere else.* Even on relatively quiet roads, a child should not be crossing the road alone till she is seven or eight.

Painting and Drawing
From as young as two or three a child can begin to use different drawing and colouring media. Let her work in her own way – there is no correct way to 'draw' with paints, pens, or crayons. There is no proper way to draw people or objects; a child finds out for herself what she is interested in doing with each medium, what can and can't be done.

Playgroup gives opportunity for painting but do have poster paints at home, using powder colours and mixing them as you need them. A washing-up liquid container may be cut in half and the top turned upside down into the bottom half. This forms a relatively spillproof container as effective as the commercial counterpart. For thick colour and economical use of paint, mix a little wallpaper paste and use this instead of water to mix the powder. Add a few drops of washing up liquid, then if the paint does get onto clothes it washes out even more easily. Odd wallpaper rolls or lining paper make good, cheap, painting paper. Some companies have waste paper from their computers; see if your friends can supply any. Once in a while it's worth finding or buying an extremely large piece of paper so your child can be really flamboyant with the paint in a mural-sized project.

Crayons, felt pens, and pencil crayons all have their own character for drawing. Felt pens are bright and cannot be blended together. Pencil crayons are subtle but as children grow they may appreciate the qualities produced.

Wax crayons have many interesting results. Take a sheet of grease-proof paper and make a crayonned picture, filling in the whole surface with solid colour, going over it several times to make it thick. Take the finished picture and paint the back thinly with cooking oil. When it has dried stick the picture to a window and you will find the light comes through much like stained glass. Use wallpaper paste to glue Christmas pictures made this way to the windows; remove them on twelfth day with hot soapy water.

Children who enjoy crayons also enjoy covering a piece of paper with layer upon layer of different colours, ending with a dark one. Scratch patterns or pictures into the resulting waxy surface and the underneath colours show through as the picture. If they make a mistake they can crayon over it.

Let your child tell you about her painting and colouring. It may be a picture of something particular or just a mass of colours drawn for fun. Always affirm the child – and perhaps you can find a place to put the pictures on the wall. Never throw away a child's handiwork or shrug it off without interest. If you have to get rid of forgotten paintings, as you can't store them, do so when your child is not there or, with an older child, ask which ones she wants to keep.

HOME SKILLS

Between the ages of three and five there are many home skills a child enjoys. As you read through those below ask yourself several questions. Which is my child already doing and what are the next steps to learning? If your child is older, ask yourself how you are now giving your child opportunity to learn in this field. For example, when a child has learned numbers, addition, and weighing, she may now be able to read recipes for herself and later be able to cope with the hot oven or make a simple meal for the family.

Cooking – A small child begins rolling and cutting pastry or biscuit dough, placing shapes on a floured tin for cooking. Before long she will be able to rub together flour and fat till it resembles breadcrumbs, a task that helps to refine the co-ordination of the child's hands, much as the baby learns to clap. Scones or cakes can be mixed if a parent does the weighing and gives the child the ingredients in the right order. Her arm may ache with mixing, but she will enjoy having made a tray of small cakes and icing them, or making them into butterflies, with butter icing.

Cleaning the sink or the bath, learning to squeeze out a cloth or sponge, learning to squeeze a little of the cleanser, are all tasks within a child's scope. Give some supervision as squeezy containers have a way of becoming wild in the hands of a small child who may be so fascinated with the effect that there will be trails of cleanser all over the bathroom. In their fascination the child will have forgotten what they were told about squeezing only a little.

Find a child-size broom, dustpan, and brush and you have a

Learning for Life

regular helper with your cleaning. Dusting can be done by a small child, though do avoid precious ornaments which may roll if not placed in a particular way. Avoid shelves over fireplaces. Buy your polish in flat tins, not aerosol cans, so there's no danger of polish being sprayed in the face of a child.

Sewing. Boys and girls can learn simple sewing tasks. If you have a selection of buttons, let them sew them onto a scrap of cloth. You can take them off afterwards to start again.

Knitting. Children, given scaled-down needles, can knit simple pieces. Cast on ten stitches and first illustrate the process to your child, going very slowly and repeating aloud the words that describe the process.

'Put the needle in,
 Put the wool round,
 Pull the needle out (keeping the wool on it),
 Drop the old stitch off.'

If your child hasn't got the general idea after about fifteen minutes, try in a few months time, or when they ask again. Make simple scarfs for dolls and teddy bears. If your child makes squares, they can be sewn together into clothes for dolls and animals. Use a short stubby sewing needle so it is not too discouraging if they prick their fingers.

Setting a table is an interesting challenge. It is a household task but a helpful foundation for number work. Make a place for each family member, by name. For each place, your child can match up a knife, fork, and spoon, bring plates of the appropriate size as well as glasses. Give minimum help and if you want to change something your child has set, explain why, without being too bossy. Some inaccuracies at first may be left but as he or she gets older point them out, like knife and fork at the wrong side or individually the wrong way round. By the way, many small children are ambidextrous but if they are proving to be left-handed don't try to change this.

Laundry. Let your child wash doll's and teddy's clothes by hand, wringing them out and hanging them on the line to dry. Washing, rinsing and all the other stages can be fun, especially in fine weather when they can have a bowl of water in the garden for their work. Fix up a low string for a washing line which is easier to reach than the high one used for the family wash. You may want to show how you use your washing machine, but it is best to leave this till she is ten or so.

Gardening. Even if you have only a tiny garden let children help with the work, the digging, planting and harvesting. If possible give a child a small patch of her own; even a square metre can have lots of plants in it. Annuals are the best as far as flowers go. Root vegetables are very rewarding, as well as lettuce or tomato plants. They may wish to take some pocket money to a Garden Centre where they can buy such plants singly. Mustard and cress can be grown on the window ledge along with other pot plants.

Shopping. When you go to the supermarket tell your child what you are looking for and she can help, recognising the colour and shape before being able to read the labels. See if she recognises the size you usually buy. Until she can count money in a couple of years time she cannot be much more than an observer at the check-out.

Woodworking. Hammers and nails are useful when scraps of wood are available. At first your child won't make machines, boxes or useful items, but will just hammer in nails for fun and join wood together without order. However, if she works with wood when a parent is mending or making, she may want to make a product with a particular use.

When the postman calls it is exciting to get a letter. Post one to your child. Get relatives and friends to post direct to your child so she can grasp the idea of mail and can send her own pictures to grandparents as a greeting.

Encourage those who phone to speak direct to your child if they are asking her round to play. They can then check it out with parents. This way, handling the phone for her own business, she will become proficient at dealing with messages. However, be cautious about allowing a child to answer the phone by herself. Some manage well but others forget to fetch the adult that the caller asked for and leave the phone off the hook with a very frustrated caller. Wait until she is older before you allow her to dial unsupervised as mistakes can be quite costly.

The skills acquired in early childhood equip a child to be both self-sufficient and helpful. Biblical patterns of learning involved working alongside parents, though by Jesus's time boys were receiving some schooling.

Learning in the family tends to include attitudes as well as techniques. In a family setting a child is as generous with what she makes as her parents are generous. If parents give joyfully and unconditionally children will copy. Alongside them they may learn to be industrious or hardworking. All this happens as the family, parents and children, work alongside one another in the home and garden.

Learning for Life

At school, with such attitudes already established in the early years, the child will learn more of information and techniques, such as weighing and measuring. At home those skills can be used in the give and take of family life. It is at home too that the child learns the most important lessons that surround skills, of personal and relationship values which can tell us how, when and why to use our knowledge.

An important example for today's children is the subject of sex education. Schools are criticised for being clinical in their teaching, even when the teaching states that the context for sexual intercourse is marriage. At home, conversations and the quality of the relationship between the child's parents, their faithfulness, openness and care for one another, are by far the strongest illustration of a sexual relationship in the context of love and commitment. In this sense the home is again adding the spiritual dimension of the quality of life for children.

QUESTIONS FOR INDIVIDUALS AND GROUPS

1. Make a note of home skills you remember learning from your parents. Note also how you learned them.
2. Think of your child/children and the opportunities you have taken to work together so they may learn from working with you.

If your children do not normally work with you, why is this?

Could there be significant reasons for you to get them working with you sometimes?

QUESTIONS FOR GROUPS

1. Tell each other about your notes from the individual questions, especially about how you learned as children.
2. Discuss together whether it is even necessary for children to learn home skills from their parents. If so, how are your children learning them? Pool ideas.
3. Are there opportunities in the church for children to work alongside adults? List them. Can you add others or make further opportunity for your children?
4. Read together the story of Mary and Martha, Luke 11:38–42. Why do you think that Luke included this story? Does it communicate any particular values with regard to children learning life-skills? In thinking of yourselves, which members of the group are more like Martha and which members are more like Mary? Has this affected your discussion of the characters and the teaching?

8. EDUCATIONAL SKILLS

Many parents attempt to start their children on educational skills before the children begin school, believing that the child is ready to learn new skills and will be given a better start at school if she knows how to read and write before she gets there. The former assessment may be correct but the latter is seldom of significance. Your child's first teacher puts her through all the foundational work for reading and writing when she arrives in the reception class. Why? Because the foundations for these skills are many and varied, and unless the child has integrated them, her development will be hampered by being pushed into more advanced skills too soon. Educational success does not come from being able to do something first and fastest, but in breadth of experience and understanding.

LEARNING SKILLS

There are myriads of tasks that are done at home that support the learning principles to be undertaken later in school.

Right and left. Help your child know which hand is which. Do her gloves have a right and left hand? Wellington boots can be on the wrong feet. Help her know which is which. When you're on the bus or in a car talk about turns to left and right so children can distinguish between them.

Colours. Some are learned more readily than others; the easiest is red. Talk about colours when putting on clothes, looking at pictures, finding packets. Don't immediately try out subtle colours but first point out the more distinct or primary colours: red, yellow, green, black, white and blue. It is enough initially to recognise the shades under one general name.

Matching is an endlessly helpful pre-school skill. If you have a box of assorted buttons your child may sit for a long time sorting them, finding colours, numbers of holes and different sizes. They can be sorted into a couple of empty margarine tubs. Most homes have a place in the kitchen into which the family drops paper clips, odd buttons, bits of string, screws, plugs, playing pieces from games, all sorts of little things that you don't want to lose. Ask your child to sort these out for you and put them where they belong. This involves collecting related things together and finding their proper place. These are real life ways to tackle a task she is given at school, learning to match by colour, shape, and size, essential ground work for learning number and quantity.

Jigsaws require matching shape as well as colour and are a helpful pre-reading skill. There are some where shapes such as animals fit into a specially shaped hole in a picture and others are more conventional. Try them all. Give tips and encouragement but avoid taking over and doing the task for her. Look again at the messages in chapter one; don't fall into the habit of taking over so teaching a child to expect to fail.

Some simple games, like *Snap* and *Happy Families*, work on matching principles. Others depend on collecting or making up a complete animal, such as a bear. Packs and boxes usually have an age recommendation on them. If you get one and your child is not interested or can't get the hang of it, put it away for a few weeks and try again.

Weighing. If you have scales that have weights (rather than a scale pan with a dial) a child can 'weigh' buttons or beans into paper bags, experimenting with how much it takes to tip the scales. Don't tell her how to experiment or what she is supposed to discover.

Scrapbooks involve cutting and sticking pictures. Colour magazines, catalogues, postcards, and birthday cards can all go into the collection.

Construction kits and bricks are important tools to conceptualising shape and size. The relation between various pieces and their functions develops a child's perception as well as encouraging hand and eye co-ordination. A building set such as Lego, while being expensive, has the advantage of being well-made and can be expanded as the child grows. You may find an older child who is prepared to pass on their set, so you don't have an enormous outlay of money, or look for them at jumble sales and second-hand shops.

Children of all ages up to early teens enjoy making models out of left-over cardboard boxes, packages, cylinders, plastic containers and other general junk. Keep a collection of empty packages, string, and tape, and on some rainy days bring these out for your child to work with. Suggest a monster or a machine to make on the odd chance she has no ideas. She may wish to paint her creation. Inventions are always encouraging as a child takes an idea she has in mind and tries to produce a 'real' one.

Free use of materials in creative design and construction prepare children for interest in science and technology. The intricacies of construction, of fitting tiny detail, of discovering suitable materials for the task, of finding adhesive that can actually stick this material, prepare children to have a creative approach to a future work in industry.

Clay and all sorts of tactile materials can be used. Have clay, plasticine, and playdough. Each has its own textural qualities so don't always provide the same one. Try clay from a craft shop, keeping it damp in an airtight container.

Playdough is simply made by mixing one cup of flour with half a cup of salt; mix to stiff dough with water. In an airtight container it keeps for a few days. Playdough can be moulded into shapes, hardened on a radiator or in a very low oven, painted and varnished. In this way a child can make dolls' house food or nativity models for Christmas. The items should be made quite small or they break too easily while drying.

Collect a miscellany of small items, leaves, seeds, shells, and make a collage, glueing them into a pattern on a piece of paper. Similarly, dried seeds and pulses from the larder can be used.

If you can have a sandpit in the garden this is ideal, if not find one you can visit. Some play parks have one. Cover your sandpit at night, so the cats don't use it as a toilet. Let your child make mud pies with water and old containers or with seaside buckets and spades. She will enjoy digging holes, mixing, and moulding in the garden in a space between the plants. Dress her for the occasion in clothes in which she know it is fine to get dirty.

Stories are an invaluable contribution that parents can make. Experience of handling books and listening to stories is an enormous asset to learning. Given a selection of books at home and the addition of visits to the bookshop and library your child begins to grasp the idea of books. They stimulate the imagination and extend her world into unknown and imaginary places. Children get the idea that the picture tells the story and later that the words you read are fixed in the little black shapes that cross the page. She also finds that the story stays the same because the written words and the pictures are fixed. The story stays inside the book too. It doesn't come out into the 'real' world.

Pictures. Throughout early years the child adds to her speaking vocabulary, her ability to name objects she sees and in her use of descriptive words and verbs. However, it is always helpful to spend time looking at pictures, allowing your child to take a lead in talking about what she sees. Ask questions and give information if necessary. Such times can fill in gaps in the child's knowledge, names of male and female animals, the names and uses for tools, sporting actions, relationship names, colours. She will also learn to describe what she sees, an important prelude to descriptive and creative writing.

Conversation. Encourage your child to tell her own stories about what she has done and seen during the day. These prepare the child for the complex task of linking writing skill with having something to say.

In conversations, help children to listen to others, learn to follow simple instructions methodically, and to take messages. She may take a message out to a parent in the garden or in another room, even as simple as telling her a meal is ready. It could be a question with an answer to be carried back.

Nursery rhymes and songs teach rhythm, rhyme, and simple music. Introduce your child to music and making sounds with all sorts of home-made instruments. Help her listen to various types of music which she may enjoy dancing to.

Avoid counting objects or trying to get your child to add up, though you may teach her to reel off numbers in order, just like nursery rhymes. Also avoid reading, especially phonetically. You might want to help a child recognise her own name, written with an initial capital letter with the rest lower case, thus: **Joanne**. The whole word should be recognised without breaking it into individual letters.

If you do use the occasional written word, never use capitals, always lower case letters.

If in doubt, don't. Even if you think you are sure, ask her prospective school and class teacher first or you may do more harm than good. Trying to start a child too soon on recognising words or numbers can result in a word blindness that is a problem for a long time; those early attempted words may be blanks in the child's mind that will cause confusion.

QUESTIONS FOR INDIVIDUALS AND GROUPS

1. Check through your child's toys and books. Do they encourage learning? Are there obvious gaps?

Educational Skills

2. How many of the skills listed in the chapter above, has your child tackled? What could you add?

QUESTIONS FOR GROUPS

1. As well as the many practical life skills your children need, there is a helpful biblical instruction about their education. Read the following passages, which show how concerned Moses was, and he was prophesying here, that the people help their children understand their life, Deuteronomy 4:10–14; 6:4–9 and 32:46–47. Consider together the things that it is important for you to tell your children, so they grow up aware of themselves as God's people.

2. Can church education in Sunday School help children with these skills?

How does church education fit into the overall picture of a child's education? Discuss the aims and purposes of church programmes and what you would like them to achieve for your children.

9. STARTING SCHOOL

The first day at school is a major step for a five-year-old. Starting school is as hard as the first day of the first job, and as frightening as moving to a country that speaks a different language. So much is different: organisation, structure, the size of the group, the schedule, the purpose, and the relationships. Playgroup helps in the transition from home to school for many children, helping five-year-olds take it in their stride after a short initial time of confusion at the differences. Nevertheless, parents can help prepare for this new adventure in several ways.

Attending playgroup helps a child with being away from home for a number of hours under the care of another adult. The level of supervision provided in a playgroup gives a higher

Starting School

staff-to-child ratio than is true in school, while the child becomes used to other caring adults.

Playgroup introduces a child to play with others her own age. Every child goes through three stages of play; first playing alone, close to, but uninvolved with a friend; next playing a game within which they each do their own activity, such as with a sand-table; then choosing play in which friends are interdependent. These stages take time and occur in school if there has been no previous opportunity.

When there are still some months to go before the child starts school begin specific preparations to help her. Assuming that she has been accepted for it, begin pointing out the particular school to your child. Give her time to watch through the fence, so she can see the children and the classrooms, adjusting to the idea of this particular place.

There are things to be talked about together. The most important people when a child begins school are her class teacher and the infant helpers who work in her class, and possibly the head teacher.

Explain that the teacher is the person who looks after the children, organises and helps them. Explain that she will set them projects and activities to do, as well as giving them time to play. Sometimes all the children are asked to do something together, more often they are in small groups around a table, with the teacher helping them get started, whether on drawing, colouring or other activity. 'She will help and there's no need to be afraid that you won't understand, she will be happy to explain to you again.'

Reception class teachers seem to have a special gift for helping children through the first few days and weeks till they are comfortable in the new environment. They are extremely patient, tolerant and sympathetic so give the child a picture of a friendly helpful teacher. The teacher knows that every child adjusts differently and at different speeds. She makes allowances for this and encourages them on as they are ready for new work.

Some schools operate an excellent system in which each class has mixed ages, for example, five-to-seven-year-olds in one class together. This is specially helpful to beginners in school. They find themselves mixed in with other children who know the routines and show them how to get started on work. The older children still remember the feeling of the first day and are very helpful if a smaller child is confused or cries. They look after the younger ones in the playground. This is an obvious help to the teacher who can ask an older child to help tie shoelaces, or undertake other simple caring tasks. It is comforting for a child to arrive among a group of friendly children who already know how to cope, and the newer ones very quickly copy.

Explain that there are other children and classes in the school as the numbers at school, especially on the playground, can be daunting. If your child does not adjust in a few days, see the class teacher who will find some way to help her, perhaps having an older child look after her at playtime for a while.

Older brothers or sisters, relatives or friends in the school, can walk in with a younger child, helping her to learn what to do, and showing her where to put her coat and lunchbox.

Routine

Explain the new routine to your child. Tell her that you will take her to the school gate every day.

For the first few days accompany her right to the classroom. Later, your child will realise most parents only go to the gate with their children and will want to be left there also. By the way, arrive at school with a couple of minutes to spare each day. Don't be late; some children are absolutely mortified to find themselves arriving after everyone else has started work.

A child should know *exactly* where she will be met when it's time to go home again. Always be there on time otherwise she may panic and do something unwise, such as going home alone. If a parent cannot be there, arrange in advance for someone else known to your child to be there and let your child know, even if that means phoning or sending a message to the school. She *should* refuse to accompany a stranger or an acquaintance unless you or the class teacher has specifically told her to do so. An older child, if sensible and careful, can bring home a younger brother or sister on occasions.

Playtime usually happens on three occasions during the day: mid-morning, mid-afternoon, and for part of the lunch break. The teacher will tell the children when it's playtime, lunchtime or going home time. Usually children have a piece of fruit, a biscuit or a bag of crisps for the morning playtime. There may be a water fountain available but your child may wish to take a drink. There are small attache-case lunch boxes on the market, with their own drinking bottle and cup included; most children seem to have these, so expect your child to ask for one. Make favourite and nourishing lunches as children are quite hungry after a hard morning of work and play. Most also want something to eat and drink the minute they get home.

Infant and First schools normally arrange for a child to be able to visit the class room the term before she starts attending. Other children may show the new children round. Take a good look around, see where the toilets are, how the tables are arranged, where coats are hung, where the lunchboxes are placed till lunchtime and so on. Take down the name of the teacher so your child can get used to it. Find out which way your child is to come in on the first day, straight to the classroom or through a main entrance.

On this visit or on the first day of the school term, the school secretary may ask for further details of your child for the school's records, date of birth and other relevant information.

Help
It can all be rather a lot to take in. So let your child know she can ask for help by talking to the teacher. She can also ask for an explanation if she can't follow the teacher's instructions easily.

Never threaten a child with school. If she misbehaves at home, the school cannot be expected to sort this out. It is your responsibility. Help your child be obedient before she gets there. If it is obvious that your child is naughtier at home than at school it may be worth asking the teacher about her methods of keeping order.

Children who have just started school are often extremely tired. Some schools start children on mornings-only for the first term, for this reason. But take notice; your child may need an earlier bedtime for a while and more attention in the late afternoon, the reassurance of being with mum or dad quietly after a hectic day. Look for activity together that is refreshing and peaceful. Go for a walk or relax outside, tell stories by the fire. Avoid television as this often increases tension and requires concentration and the result is a grumpy and irritable child. School often involves long periods of sitting and being still, so some free play and running around is ideal. Some children ask for more affection, for signs that they are still loved even though they are now away from parents for more of the time.

SELF-ESTEEM AT SCHOOL

The most beneficial gift your child can receive for her education is self-esteem. Build into her life a sense of achievement, of being pleased with what she has done. She can expect more of herself in the future, aware that the world has broadening horizons. She can have a sense that effort is worthwhile if she gets a warm response when she has worked hard and done her best.

At first your child may not be able to tell you what she has done at school each day. Although she cannot describe it, she may be able to show you. She may even say she played all day. Before uttering a single word of disapproval, horror, or a suggestion that children should be working, doing numbers and sums and not playing, reconsider the chapter above on foundations for learning. The child won't know that the matching or balancing was more than a game, but almost all classroom materials have a structure that includes essential learning.

Children are normally allowed to talk quietly while they work. Often they encourage one another. There is very little competition in a healthy classroom environment; the teacher does not mind when one child helps another. Teachers seldom use criticism or punishment in the learning process as they realise the effect is too often counter-productive. Most give messages that help a child see that she could do better, if the work is not as good as it could be. Don't attempt to nag or criticise a child about school work. When unsure about what a child has told them, parents can best make an appointment to see the teacher.

In the early years in particular children bring home everything from paintings and models to writing and number books. Look through them and encourage your child to tell you about them. Are there pen markings from the teacher? What do they mean? Read the stories she has written, or accounts of how she spent the weekend and from them learn how she perceives family life. Some of the stories will be very imaginative; on other days she may have felt quite unlike writing and the effect is uninspired work. Don't worry – everyone has good and bad days.

The boy who lives next door to me found that writing his diary each Monday at school was boring after uneventful weekends. On such occasions he created fictional weekends, things he wished he had done. His skill has developed over several years and he is now planning a twenty-page adventure story with several chapters.

Parents tend to worry about 'standards' far more than is necessary. Teachers may put a gold star on a piece of work because they like it or to encourage a child for effort or when the work is specially good. Sometimes on a special day everyone gets a gold star. Don't get too worried at more or less gold stars, you may be taking them more seriously than teacher and pupil.

Once a child starts reading she often brings home her reading book for a parent to listen to her read a couple of pages. The more practice a child gets with reading, the better. As it's impossible for the teacher to listen to all of her class every day teachers count on the parents' involvement.

Learning to read starts with the shape of whole words. At first the child is memorising the whole shape of 'dog' or 'father'. So as a child is just beginning to read, perhaps has a vocabulary of five to fifty words, tell her the complete word rather than trying to build it from sounds. Learning phonetically, by building up from individual letters, comes a year or so later after she has learned the shapes and sounds of individual letters. If there seems to be considerable difficulty, ask the teacher for advice.

When a child brings home a painting or model, find out how it was made and how it works. Sometimes pictures are illustrations of stories heard in the class. Ask about the story.

Find out about the other children, especially new-found friends. Parents ought not attempt to influence a child's choice of friends. She has all kinds of reasons for playing with different children and it is unwise and unkind to other children for parents to steer her away from ones *they* don't like. Friendships, and the quality of friendship, are something everyone discovers for themselves. As a child learns trust and self-respect at home she will choose friends who are trusting and caring, who treat their friends with respect.

When a child has learned to write her name encourage her with opportunities to write it at home, on the bottom of a picture or on a letter to grandmother. When she begins to write for herself let her ask for help if she needs it; she won't want too much intrusion from others.

Up to the age of seven or more almost all children write particular letters and numbers back to front. Ask the teacher if your child should be told that they have got letters the wrong way.

Most children are not asked to write within lines in the early stages; letters and numbers tend to become more orderly with experience. If you write something for your child to copy, use lower case letters, as near as possible to the style the teacher uses. Many learn a very simple style similar to that found in Ladybird Books, so use that as an example of style.

Sometimes problems in reading and writing can be caused by eye and hand co-ordination. These may change with physical growth and simply disappear, or a child may receive extra help in a 'special' or 'remedial' group.

LEARNING DIFFICULTIES

There are many reasons why a child may experience learning difficulties at school. Some may be temporary, when there's an upset at home or during a time of transition. Those resulting from a permanent handicap are going to be with the child all her life. A number of children are slow learners because of their intelligence quotient, and are not high achievers academically. Some personalities are interested in practical subjects and crafts and are never as interested in the more theoretical or academic subjects. Yet every child has potential to develop and should have an optimum environment to do this.

Starting School

Making the best out of opportunities at school relates to more than just academic skills. These learning years provide opportunity for social, emotional and physical development too. The parents as well as the teacher can look out for signals that a child is not at her best and decide together how to help. It is important in this field, almost more than any other, that the teacher and the parents recognise that they are in partnership, providing every opportunity and help to the child's growth.

Slowness

Sometimes a child with considerable potential for academic skills, reading and arithmetic, is not doing so well as she could. Talk this over with the teacher and look at the problem as a family.

Does the child have enough sleep? Is she lethargic because she is tired? Try an earlier bedtime for a while. Perhaps she is the youngest and tends to go to bed at a time that suits older sisters and brothers rather than the child herself.

Also look at diet. Does she have a balanced diet?

Consider the time spent watching TV. Often in a busy family a child can be watching for many hours a week without the total being noticed. For the next week of school make a note each day of the time the TV goes on and the time it goes off. What is the total? Television is a very passive occupation. How much personal time and attention has the child had over the same period? What was her mood after the TV was turned off? Keep a record of this also for a few days.

A child who is slow in being interested in reading may be helped by spending more time in the family listening to stories, chatting and playing games. Over a few weeks a child may suddenly get the hang of books and reading, through even a few minutes extra attention each day. Try outings to the library, so new and interesting stories can be included. Talk together and tell stories for your child and encourage her to make up stories to tell others.

Shyness

It is often recognised that the child who is too quiet may need just as much help as the over-noisy or aggressive child. It is unnatural to be withdrawn and fearful, damaging the child's ability to make friends. If a child tends to hang back fearfully from other children, find out what the problem is. For a child who has not attended playgroup before starting school, being in a busy, noisy crowd of children is frightening and she can be slow to join in. Give encouragement by helping the child know what is happening if she is confused. At home it is easier to have a quiet word to find out what she is afraid of and let the teacher know so she can help sort any problems. She may introduce the child to other children. The teacher may also seat her at a table with quieter children, as even the natural boisterousness of the confident ones may make a child feel worse about herself and her inability to cope with the pace.

Shyness can slow down a child's learning as she hesitates rather than asking a question, being silent rather than getting help. The result can be gaps in learning that may not show up immediately.

Aggression

Parents are more likely to hear from someone, usually a teacher, if their child is being over-aggressive or hurting other children.

Firstly, it is necessary to stop any violent or over-bossy behaviour. The child's friendships, both now and in the future, will be hurt if it continues. She must respect other children. Make an absolute rule that the child may not fight other children, however much she thinks this is justified.

Secondly, find out why she is reacting aggressively. Does she try to make everyone do what she tells them? Help her see, by talking to her, that friends are people who enjoy doing things together in a way they both choose.

Pushing other people around ends up with them refusing to play with an aggressive child. If it is apparent that she strikes out because she can't cope with teasing or bullying on the playground, ask the teacher to help. She will talk to the class about behaving differently; this can be very effective with younger children.

Among a group of five-year-olds was one very determined girl, Jane. During playtime Jane began to hit the other children in the small group. I brought her out of the group, to talk to me, help me understand why she felt it necessary to hit other children. She was crying with frustration, 'They won't do what I tell them to do!' 'Perhaps they don't want to do it, Jane.' She was silent for a moment. 'But the game won't work if they don't do it!' 'Do they want to play the game your way?' 'I want them to.' We talked for a while and I told Jane that she could go back to playing with the other children when she was ready to play without hitting anyone. If she found they weren't listening, she must not hit them. I would like her instead to fetch me so I could help her think about how to talk to them. She sat with me for a while before telling me she was ready to play without hitting and I allowed her to rejoin the group. Jane was an only child who, unlike the other children who were together that morning, had had little experience of negotiating with others: she needed opportunity to discover ways of talking with her peers, and some help from her teachers to keep her from alienating herself from them by expressing her frustration violently.

Sometimes a child is aggressive when she arrives home from school, after being well-behaved all day. For most children school is a fairly hard and demanding world and a child wants to let off steam somewhere. Stop her being aggressive with the other children and instead spend time with her when she arrives home, helping her to express feelings without hurting anyone. Having a parent's complete attention, quietly and unhurriedly, can give a child her first chance in a busy day to tell someone how she feels and what she thinks. (Look at **Active Listening** on page 20.)

Minor handicaps
Large numbers of children have minor handicaps, which affect learning.

There are regular medical check-ups during a child's school career. Use these as opportunities for asking questions about minor problems. Eyesight and hearing are tested and recommendations are made by the school doctor if necessary. Similarly a school dentist checks on the children, advising further treatment if necessary.

Slight deafness can delay learning various skills as the child misses explanations. A medical check-up should identify the problem and if necessary a child will be equipped with a hearing-aid.

Similarly sight problems may first be apparent when the child tries to read the blackboard from the back of the class. Of course, she has no idea she is seeing less well than anyone else so won't tell parents or teacher. The teacher may be the first to notice.

Major handicaps
Many children are born with handicaps that necessitate their being given special education. Each and every child must be carefully assessed to discover the best form of education for her. Many times this begins in the home long before the child reaches school age. While initial contacts for help for the parents of a handicapped child may come through doctors and local hospital specialists, much can be gained from meeting parents of other handicapped children. The National Children's Bureau[1] is a central agency bringing together people who are involved in many forms of childcare, professionals in teaching, nursing, family support and research foundations. Through this organisation parents may contact others in a similar situation and discover the range of help available for the handicapped child.

It would be impossible in a general book on children to comprehensively consider the educational and health needs of the handicapped so I will make no attempt to do so.

It is helpful for parents whose children are not handicapped to be aware of the problems and pressures of handicaps. Many churches are able to welcome members with various handicaps and so become conscious of the problems that are related to their lives. Local authorities are more often attempting to educate handicapped children in special units attached to local schools, in order to reduce the alienation that can be the result of specialised but separate education.

Just recently a friend, Elizabeth, who works with the handicapped, told me a story. A young girl on coming home from school asked if her friend (I will call him Jamie) could come home with her from school the next day, to play and have tea. Her mother thought that a good idea. Upon hearing this the girl began to tidy the room. 'It's really not too untidy,' began the mother as the girl began to move the chairs as well. 'I have to move things, you see Jamie is special.' This explanation meant nothing to the mother until further explanations revealed that Jamie had a wheelchair.

The careful introductions that the school had given the children in his class about Jamie, helped the other children to accept him as a friend and encouraged them to ease the effects of his disability. While it is often said that young children can be very unkind to those who are 'different', once the hurtful effect of their words is pointed out and they are shown how to be more caring, most children show incredible kindness and consideration.

VISITING SCHOOL

Recognition of the importance of parents and teachers working together has resulted in more opportunities for parents to visit their child's school and talk to teachers. Parents are made aware of their child's projects and tasks, so they can support and encourage her. Some of today's parents grew up with schools that tended to be authoritarian, to use fear as a means of control and to discourage any parental approach to teachers. Hard though it may be to forget that, approach teachers as friends and co-workers. Where there are difficulties avoid speaking with anger or hostility. A parent with such strong feelings should see the head teacher first, explaining the sense of hurt and asking for clarification and assistance. A class teacher who is approached by an angry and aggressive parent naturally withdraws. It is extremely destructive to a child's education for parent and teacher to be at loggerheads. Speak to her of recognising the difficulty, without accusing her of incompetence or neglect. A parent who knows how to help the child's response and so help the teacher in the classroom, can make such a suggestion. 'I hear from John that things have not been very smooth just recently. May I make a suggestion about how I deal with John when something like this is happening.'

Open Evening
Open Evening comes in two forms. Some schools place all sorts of work on display for an evening and invite parents to visit the school, meeting teachers in an informal atmosphere. There is usually little chance to raise specific questions, so make notes

of any questions to ask when there is a more appropriate opportunity to raise them.

Another reasonably common form is for parents to visit the school while the children are working. Parents get a taste of the general atmosphere of the school, and meet the rest of their child's class. It is possible to see some teaching in progress and to make contact with the school staff.

Parents Evening
Once each academic year parents are usually invited to an evening of appointments at which time they may ask very specific questions about their child's progress. (Most schools send an annual report home as well). There are several important areas to be covered in conversation with teachers, and make notes as the teacher responds to specific questions, especially of areas that could be helped by parents.

How is your child's general behaviour? Is she on the whole co-operative and ready to follow instructions? Is she helpful?

Some children are very talkative; it's only worth worrying about this if your child is chatting so much she can't get her work done. Apart from that, chatter can be helpful, giving a child opportunity to verbalise thoughts before writing.

How is your child getting on with other children? Does she have friends and is she able to keep up with them? Is your child apparently a loner or isolated?

Expect every child to have at least one or two friends and be able to mix reasonably with other children. If your child is too often alone she may need encouragement. The teacher may have suggestions about how to talk to your child.

What is the standard of your child's work? Aspects of behaviour affect a child's work standard. Be sure to get a picture of those first.

For various aspects of the curriculum, ask how your child is progressing?

Mathematics. What sort of work is she doing and how is she coping with it? How can you help or encourage her? If the teacher mentions an aspect of modern maths which is outside your experience ask her for the name of the book in which you can find out about it.

Reading. What level has she reached? Is your child interested and sure of what she is doing? What kind of help might you give at home? What kinds of books should you be getting from the library or buying for presents?

Writing. Is your child doing as well as she can? Is her work neat? Has she grasped the general idea? How is she managing with creative writing? Is there anything she should be doing at home to help with work?

Crafts. Find out about your child's skills and interests. The teacher may well have suggestions. Some children are so concerned at not getting dirty that they won't really enjoy the messier crafts. Your child may need reassurance – and a craft apron to help her keep as clean as she wants to be. When considering presents for birthday or Christmas, are there particular types of craft materials that the school would recommend for their creative value, and which kinds would they recommend you avoid?

Projects. Most primary schools work on projects and interests rather than clear definitions between such subjects as geography and history. It's more likely that your child is, for example, studying winter and in that context considers weather, the world's seasonal patterns, clothing, and a variety of related topics. Ask the teacher to tell you about your child's project work and how different disciplines are included.

Most teachers are dedicated to the children in their care, going out of their way to help and encourage them. Many teachers design work for particular children according to their need and interest. *Always* thank the teacher for her interest in your child, telling her how you appreciate her work.

Appointments

If a child is showing signs of stress about school or if parents have a particular worry about their child during the year and this cannot wait for a parents' evening, ask the teacher for a special appointment.

If there is to be a major change at home that could affect a child's work or attitudes, let his teacher know. A new baby, moving house, a divorce, a major illness could all affect the child's performance.

If a child is ill for more than a day or two parents may wish to find out how to help her catch up with her work.

HELPING THE SCHOOL

The overall quality of life or atmosphere at a school has a significant effect on the morale of children and teachers, affecting the children's learning. There is usually opportunity for parents to become involved in the life of the school through a Parent-Teacher Association. Many facilities that are helpful to schooling cannot be provided out of funds from the local authority; there is insufficient money. Working together, parents and teachers are able to undertake fund raising and specific improvement projects. Such groups have worked to stop schools from being closed, to campaign for a sixth form, to raise money for a swimming pool, to help supervise swimming sessions during the holidays, to redecorate classrooms, to pay for new books for the library. Ask for information at the school.

If there is no PTA there may be occasional letters from the head teacher asking for help on Summer Fairs and Fetes and inviting parents to come to spend their money.

School staff cannot always cover all aspects of the daily running and some schools have a parent to help with running the library, playground supervision or as helpers in the classroom.

There are occasional opportunities for parents to assist in supervision of school outings and holidays. It is necessary to understand the responsibility of supervision, to know the kinds of places to be visited and any possible danger the children might meet. Many local authorities have, or are working on, guidelines for school trips. Find out about these or ask the head teacher for some training, before you go.

There is provision for several representatives of parents of children in the school to be on the School Governors. By this means parents have contact with various aspects of policy and order of the school and some access to the appointment of staff. A letter is sent to all parents offering them opportunity to vote for their choice, usually enclosing a short introductory letter from each nominee, so you know what they stand for. The Open University has produced a course for Parent Governors[2] so they can examine the principles and tasks involved in the work.

QUESTIONS FOR INDIVIDUALS AND GROUPS

1. Remembering back to your own school days, note down the aspects that through your observation appear to have changed the most over the intervening years. Try listing ten aspects.

Are you puzzled about why these changes have taken place? If you are, use your next visit to the school as an opportunity to find the answers. Alternatively you may have a friend who is a teacher who could help.

2. Look back at the suggestion for keeping a diary of your

child's television viewing. Ensure that you undertake this for the next three days. Keep note of the hours watched, the particular programmes watched and also the child's mood at the end. Did you have to interrupt his watching for mealtimes or bedtimes?

Are there any changes that you would like to make? [There is a fuller assessment of the effects of television, in chapter seventeen.]

3. How are you making time with your child for the reading and memorising that he brings home from school with him?

Can you see progress? How is the time you spent of positive help for your child?

4. There are many experiences in life of which we are afraid. Look at the story of Jonah, and the story of Elijah. There are many responses in them, some are negative: for example, Elijah seems to have been afraid after God had taken up the sacrifices, and looked for a safe place. Children's response to the life change involved in starting school can often be shock. Do these and other Bible stories give you ideas of how to help and encourage your child?

QUESTIONS FOR GROUPS

1. Take considerable time to go over the individual responses above.

Talk over the changes in schooling, and where you think the change is negative, prepare a suitable set of questions and invite a local head teacher to come and talk to you about the aims of education.

Talk over the questions of TV time, especially about who decides the order and scheduling of family life: parents, children or TV, or a careful balance of all three.

Are some children having specific problems with which other members of the group can help, for example with reading?

2. Are there major projects for children particularly needed in the school, church or neighbourhood? Are you able to offer assistance? If there is no action group can you form one, or can you add yourselves to an existing one?

Footnotes
[1] The National Children's Bureau, 8 Wakley Street, London, EC1V 7QE.

[2] Further information about the School Governors Course is available from The Open University, PO Box 48, Walton Hall, Milton Keynes, MK7 6AB.

10. SCHOOL DAYS

The years during which a child is growing through infant and junior stages at school and before she reaches adolescence are in many ways the most stable of times, yet these are years of rapid growth and development. The child acquires new social and physical skills and is established in the daily routine of the bigger world that is provided in the school setting.

The pre-school years, often turbulent for parents and children, settle into new stability before the emotional and social turmoil of early teens. Between the ages of six and eleven the parents' chief role with their child is support, enjoyment and encouragement. On the whole, patterns of discipline and order in family life settle into a routine that is both less dominated by the pressing demands of a baby or toddler, and more easily adapted as family needs change. Increasingly parents and children become friends, having hobbies and interests in common, discussing common interests and enjoying one another's company.

DEVELOPING SKILLS

When a child starts school as a five-year-old she spends the majority of her time in the classroom acquiring the skills that enable her to learn for herself. Reading, writing and arithmetic, commonly called the 3 R's, are the groundwork for future understanding. The first three years result in a child's ability to read for herself. Choose fiction books appropriate to her skills and interests; select informative non-fiction books when they need relevant facts. In the library and the bookshop your child can make her own selections. She begins to be able to read signs in shops and on streets.

The child is equipped for pursuing her own interests. Once a child can read the clock as well as the words on the page encourage her to read the TV Times and not turn on the set to find out what's on.

Most seven-to-eight-year-olds are fairly confident in their use of the written word and are able to communicate their thoughts in writing. Some may write letters, others may more confidently write a diary or report of their day, or enjoy creative writing, making up their own stories. Despite continued struggles with spelling, most have reached the stage of mastering the written word, and are able to use it as they wish.

Encourage your child by using written forms, let her make the shopping list as she is told what is needed this week. Let her choose and send cards and presents, addressing envelopes as well as writing the message.

As a child has opportunity to use language so her vocabulary, understanding, and ability to communicate grow. She has a wide listening vocabulary, she hears words and knows their meaning, but speaking vocabulary grows only as the child has opportunity to use the words herself. In conversations with parents and other adults her sentences become more sophisticated as she develops the ability to put thoughts into words. Watching television, or reading books increases a child's listening vocabulary, but mastery of language and the ability to use it well, grows with the opportunity to use words often in speaking and writing and in using them to express herself.

Children find forms of play that encourage their personal development. Children use drama and make-believe to extend their understanding of language and relationships. As the child plays 'Mothers and Fathers', school, hospitals, she re-uses the language of those settings, making it her own. For the shy child, using puppets can be a form that brings out her ability to use language and to practise its use in a variety of roles and situations. Accept the invitation to watch the play, asking questions and joining in conversations.

In experiencing the physical environment the child gains concepts that are under the general umbrella of mathematics. The principles that make the concrete world measurable and definable are part of a child's learning experience. They learn to number and know the quantity defined by a number. She weighs a variety of items, and measures length and volume. By pouring and comparing she eventually grasps the concept of cubic measure; a pint is still a pint regardless of the shape of the container. By eleven a child has begun to realise the concepts of speed and acceleration.

Basic numerical skills for ordinary daily life become normal; counting money and working out the necessary change; adding up the cost of items on a shopping list; deciding how long a journey will take; working out fares and timetables. Often children make maps of the school and its neighbourhood, to begin to understand directions and map reading. Let a ten-year-old follow a map in the car, whether locally on familiar roads or when on a longer journey.

Physical movement
When a child first catches a ball it is with some sense of mystery, why does she sometimes end up with it in her arms and more often not. The adult patiently continues the game, knowing that sometime soon the child will realise that link between the co-ordinated movement of her hands and arms and the holding on to the ball. Playing ball with others on the playground, the child soon progresses to catching a small ball with just her hands. Almost without thinking she positions herself for catching, and by half way through primary school she is confidently taking part in team games with a ball.

Hopping poses some challenge to the pre-school child but physical co-ordination develops and the child is able to skip with a rope, using hopping and jumping actions. Primary schools often begin work on folk dancing that also develops such physical co-ordination in a social context. Children of six-plus enjoy dance and gym classes of many types, enjoy developing their own skills. The benefit is in co-ordination and body control: it is not necessarily related to future careers in dancing.

Skills in movement include developing the ability to master a variety of 'vehicles'. The stabilisers are taken off the two-wheel bike; scooters, skateboards and roller skates come into their own. Children have considerable daring, looking for new and exciting rides. Encourage them to use protective clothing for knees and elbows, and to stick to safe areas, the rinks and play areas. On the pavements children and their wheels can be a menace to pedestrians, especially if the pedestrian is a little infirm, or if he is old or disabled.

Self reliance
During these growing years the child also acquires the skills for self-management. Zips, buttons and shoelaces which were once problems can now be coped with.

Children can try on clothes and know whether they fit. Changing at school, into shorts for sports or into a swimsuit is mastered.

Help a child to learn to fold clothes, iron them where necessary, put them in the drawers tidily. Teach her to hang up her coat, make her bed, polish shoes, wash her hair, without supervision. Lots of junior children make up their own school lunches and can pack their own bag for being away from home a night or two.

Begin to offer a child a chance to do these tasks alone, with a parent checking the results each time. As the task is adequately done on a number of occasions, check only occasionally or simply remind her that today she should wash her hair. Gradually less and less reminders are necessary.

Hobbies and collections

Almost all children go through a collecting stage. Your child's room houses collections of shells, stones, plastic models, cards, pictures, and any other remotely collectable items. Promoters know this and pack the toy and sweet counters with products that have cards in them or are one of a set.

Once the stage is recognised and accepted this is one of the most endearing characteristics of children of this age. Alone or with one or two friends the child spends hours poring over stamps that cover the dining table. She grumbles when interrupted in this extremely serious activity. Often a collection of shells is carefully wrapped and rewrapped in tissue, before taking pride of place on the shelf. Many adults remember with fondness their own collections; some still have them.

Discourage a child from collecting birds' eggs. If the child is curious about natural history help her to find another way to pursue the interest.

Both boys and girls enjoy sewing and knitting. Help him or her learn to use a hand sewing machine, mend and sew on patches. (Keep the use of electric machines till teens – for safety sake.) Most are fascinated by the possibilities of Fair-Isle knitting and enjoy making small sewn and knitted items for presents.

A COLLETION OF SHELLS

In school many learn to do simple stitching, embroidery and decorative work.

Children often enjoy a hobby with parents. Fishing is one hobby that is frequently passed on from parent to child. Very few boys would go fishing if they had not first gone with Dad or been encouraged by Dad. A common interest or hobby, model making, or speedway, is often the arena for developing friendship between adult and child at a stage when the child is interested in the friendship as well as the hobby.

Homework

In the higher years of the Primary school a child brings work home. She may besiege parents with a variety of questions for projects. Since the basic skills, reading and writing, have been established, teachers set project work to use the child's own sense of curiosity to take her into research for the information from a variety of sources.

When your child comes home, as the child of a neighbour did, wanting to know all about Japan, where do you start looking?

Look up the country in an encyclopaedia, but that may give limited kinds of information, population, geography and a little history. Look in a cookery book, does it have a section of Japanese recipes? Try a recipe for the family. Look in any magazines for stories and pictures.

Among the best sources of information and pictures are agencies that deal with travel and tourism. Most travel agents have some leaflets for holidays in Japan, with photos of historic and notable monuments. Contact the Tourist service at the relevant address in London. Often they can provide pictures, leaflets and posters.

Similarly for projects on topics related to transport, go to the local transport companies for brochures and posters. On one occasion while I was teaching, a local lorry driver happily described the places and goods he had delivered recently. Look for countries of origin on packages in kitchen cupboards. The child may discover how the products got to Britain.

JUDGEMENT

The younger child sees right and wrong according to a very simple set of rules. An action is right or wrong by its result. To break an object, plate or picture, leads to punishment whether the breakage was an accident or is done intentionally.

By ten or eleven years old the child can differentiate between these, becoming more discerning.

Recognise this as a growth stage and see the effect. A younger child may respond with a great sense of injustice and confusion on seeing a sister or brother go unpunished; to them the accident and the deliberate breakage are equally punishable so she feels misused.

Similarly she may show some confusion over keeping rules that she feels are quite arbitrary. In her observation of others, rules may be broken on occasions but, not discerning the difference described here, she may break rules which parents consider should never be broken.

As far as possible, explain to your child why you have acted the way you have. She may not understand at the time but she will know that you sympathise.

Conscience
Conscience, that inner voice which warns us against certain activities, continues to be formed throughout a child's growing years. It changes and develops, and may be confused and distorted by the circumstances.

As adults talk of something going against their conscience they are talking of activity and behaviour that contravenes an inner understanding of what is good and right; this is not necessarily the same as laws. One may or may not have a guilty conscience about breaking the law, but here the question of the establishing of the conscience itself is the subject.

Conscience is built out of the child's sense of what offends or damages the relationship she has with the people most important to her. It operates subconsciously, and is assimilated through experience rather than consciously learned.

Conscience as a sense of right and wrong, looking out for the rights of others or caring for those less fortunate, cannot be instilled by indoctrination or instruction methods. Attitudes grow out of a child's close relationships, adults who are important to her, often parents but also other close adults. School alone cannot teach these values to a child, though teachers may explain them. Children in the reception class of school, at five years old, already show considerable presence of what is called 'conscience'.

Recently one child explained to me wearily that she was tired of trying to keep the school rules, they were so hard to remember. In her particular home background, it was clear that rules were random and could change from day to day without any real sense of order, so the pattern of school life bore too little relationship to her home life. She was, although wishing to please, finding a lack of the inner resource that would help her fit into the system easily. She offended without knowing why or how it had happened.

If parents are *arbitrary* about discipline and instructions, the child's conscience cannot give her a sense of wariness or guilt about breaking rules. It may warn her that Mum or Dad is about to get angry this time, or even tell her that a parent is in a good mood and so she can get away with misbehaving this time.

To parents who are Christian, this is one of the most searching aspects of nurturing children. As adults seek to live out the moral and ethical standards of Christianity in the family they are very concerned to raise their children with the same values.

The years from 0 to 5 are those during which most is assimilated, with decreasing significance from then onwards. The parents' integrity is a major element in the formation of the child's conscience. A child is not born with it. Are parents consistent or arbitrary in their personal discipline, keeping to the agreements, promises and arrangements they make for themselves, the family and friends? Do parents act with fairness, justice and with due respect for the rights of other people? Are there people who are not respected? The value judgements of the parents that result in the exclusion of people for whom they have a sense of distaste, means that the child will not in future have guilty feelings at excluding those she dislikes.

This sense of conscience as it relates to self-discipline is covered in later chapters also.

ADVENTURE

Transition into school life and routine is a major change for every child. From the closeness of home in the pre-school years the child experiences a world of new routines and structures. Yet the transition is made most comfortably when the child is very sure of her relationships at home. The conversations, answering of questions and queries, and airing of fears and confusion, all enable the child to accommodate the new experiences into her existing picture of life, and cope with the change.

The pattern of school life once established remains constant throughout childhood. On this foundation children begin to look for new experience, to push their experience and boundaries into new spheres. Not all children are adventurous in the same ways.

Clubs for children include Brownies and Cubs. These organisations provide an arena for new experience. There is opportunity for play, and children can also work for badges that reinforce basic homemaking and life skills. It is normal for Brownies and Cubs to go on outings, to go camping, and undertake chores themselves. Such clubs provide for children to spend time away from home with others of the same age, in a safe environment under the supervision of other adults, but in a setting where responsibility is encouraged.

A few children simply do not like organised activity and group work of this kind. They dislike being uniformed, being in a large group, doing the 'same' as everyone else. There's no reason why they should. Let them give such clubs a try, but when it is obvious that they really do not enjoy it, they should be allowed to drop out. However, do look for alternative ways to provide them with opportunity to develop the skills a club can provide. Help a child to find ways to learn cooking skills, and good neighbourliness. Maybe your child can camp in your garden or that of friends.

New interests that the family can undertake with this age group can include visits to the theatre and to concerts. Many drama and dance companies present special performances for children and families, which are suitable in length and content for their interest and concentration span. Look out too for companies that tour with performances of puppets. Many local festivals have drama and other performances in which children are interested. Everything from medieval miracle plays, to Morris dancing.

Many children study music in school, learning the recorder or very simple instruments such as the glockenspiel. At this age a child may wish to learn a musical instrument for herself; she now has the physical co-ordination necessary and the ability to concentrate.

Developing skills result in the child's interest in swimming and sport clubs. Often contact with these may be made through the school.

By the top of Junior school children have opportunity to travel in a school party. Sometimes this is simply a local camping trip, but some schools offer travel further afield. Take every opportunity possible, as your child expresses interest. If the cost seems too high for your family to afford, very possible if you have several children or are unemployed, visit the school

School Days

and ask the headteacher if there are funds or grants to help. Many schools recognise the problem in advance and can offer some assistance with financing a trip.

QUESTIONS FOR GROUPS AND INDIVIDUALS

1. Make some notes on your own collections as a child. What was most enjoyable about them? How many of these are still interests that you have? Adults often continue to be collectors though the objects may now be antiques, glass, or ornaments of various kinds.
2. Consider the section on judgement and conscience. Can you recognise the points in your own experience at which conscience prevents certain activity?

At certain points in their adult life, Christians have found that their inner sense of guilt was preventing them reaching maturity and have sought counsel and healing. Do you have experiences like this? Check that you are not 'passing on' your own anxieties to your child.

3. Is your child very interested in belonging to clubs for activity and friendship. To which organised groups does she belong? Note down what she is learning and benefiting from in the group.

If your child is a loner and resists belonging to organisations as far as possible, list the benefits you would expect her to receive from such groups. Next to these benefits consider how she might receive these without having to belong to groups she does not enjoy.

QUESTIONS FOR GROUPS

1. Listen to one another's responses to the individual questions above.
2. Consider the aspect of conscience. Ask each person to comment on the statement 'Rules are made to be broken'. Let every member voice their personal comment before *any* discussion happens.

This is a question that may bring a quick response because individuals' consciences tell them to keep all rules. Others allow themselves to question rules or established order.

Consider together whether conscience can be wrong, to what

extent is conscience God-given, and should everyone's conscience be telling them approximately the same limits.

3. Read Luke 6: 1–5 and Luke 13: 10–17. Consider the reasons Jesus broke the rules or codes of his day. What help do these stories give us in looking at rules and conventions today?

11. FRIENDS AND RELATIONSHIPS

A five-year-old is a rather self-centred person, concerned with her own needs and interests. She makes friends rather casually; parents and teachers are far more important than friends.

Negotiation in friendships comes gradually and at times with difficulty. Younger children may be involved in bickering, spitefulness and fighting when struggling to work their games out together. In the middle junior years friendships change, though often within an established group or gang of closer acquaintances. By ten years old most children have an established best friend, in a relationship that may last right through teenage years.

However self-sufficient a child seems to be, friends are essential and the exchange that happens in a group provides important foundations for relationships, even as adults.

Within the peer group children find loyalty and consistency. These qualities develop a broader meaning than can be found in families, because friendships are *chosen*, not present by default. Among their friends a child has to learn give-and-take. In refusing to compromise and accommodate the choices of others, they find themselves with no friends. She may rationalise this with all kinds of condemnation of her peers. Help her to see where she is discouraging friends. Give a little sympathy but recognise a child's defensive statements for what they are: a sign of their own inability to be a friend – but don't make them feel condemned; show your child how she has got herself into the position and make some suggestions of how she can change.

Among a group of friends a child finds certain values are affirmed. When skipping with a rope on the playground children expect fairness of one another. When playing card and board games the group spurns cheating or dishonesty and a child who often offends is normally excluded by the circle.

As a child joins in with the games of others she discovers that all groups have norms and established ways of conducting themselves.

In joining a group the new person is tacitly accepting the norms and order of the group. A child belongs to her family even when she is obnoxious, and she is tolerated. The same behaviour in a group of children results in her being pushed out; a selfish child is marginalised. The group does not necessarily exclude a child who naturally takes a lead or even bosses them, as long as that child leads them in what they want to do anyway. If your child is being excluded by a group she wants to play with, find out the problem and not just as she sees it. Find out how to help her negotiate with others and be more aware of what they want. The child who finds herself acceptable to a group of friends is more readily able to see herself as normal.

There are types of children who consider themselves as unacceptable for reasons that parents might not anticipate. A black child adopted by a white family in a predominantly white neighbourhood *may* see herself as strange. A physically handicapped child in a wheelchair, or a spastic child may feel the odd one out. In school, teachers can often help the child find an accepting circle of friends.

The highly intelligent child may have a hidden fear of never belonging because she can find no-one who thinks as she does; going to a larger school, where she may find some friends more like herself, can reassure her that it is alright to be the way she is. Whenever a child has what *she* feels is an unacceptable disability the friendship of peers is extremely important. Help her to find a circle in which there are potential friendships. Don't do too much for the child, encourage her in the skills of

Friends and Relationships

negotiation with others, but the significance of the achievement is in finding herself acceptable apart from parents and family.

The companionship that happens in childhood, the mutuality and the acceptance by peers is as important to future adult maturity as the qualities and values in family life. Future committed relationships, such as marriage, depend on a person's ability to maintain friendship through the ups and downs of ordinary life.

DIFFERENCES

Temperament and personality play a significant part in the growing child's life. How she relates as a person colours her learning at school, her adventurousness and choice and skill in friendships.

Consider your child, or each of your children, then yourself. Put the first initial of your child's name toward the end of the line below that more nearly describes her. Then go through the chart again describing yourself.

enjoys a group	dislikes crowds
likes surprises	likes to know everything beforehand
responds to ideas	responds more to strong feelings
likes to get everything settled	likes to keep possibilities open
is quiet	is noisy
is bossy	likes to follow
likes routine	enjoys changeability
is tidy	is messy/untidy
concentrates hard	is easily distracted

There need be no value judgement in such aspects of personality. To reflect on your child's personality can help you understand her more, enable you to see things more from her point of view.

For example, you may find it frustrating that she tends to be lonely but won't join Brownies. But you find that whereas you like groups and are happy to be organised she prefers to be less ordered and actually dislikes the feeling of being in a crowd. The resolution of her loneliness may not come in the same way you would find it. Ask parents of other quiet children how their children find friends, ask your child if there are any interests or hobbies she would like to pursue that would bring her in contact with a few people. With which friend from school would she enjoy spending more time?

Boys and Girls
Boys and girls are different in their development patterns. Expect boys and girls to respond differently in learning situations and notice their friendship patterns. Boys are more likely to enjoy a gang than girls, though not uniformly. The following chart makes some interesting comparisons, it is not true in all children, and the references to ages are approximate.[1]

GIRLS		BOYS
say their first words sooner	**Talking**	

Girls		Boys
use longer sentences, are more fluent		
learn to read sooner	**Reading**	more boys than girls need remedial reading help
spell better	**Spelling**	are not so good
learn to count at an earlier age	**Counting**	learn to count later than girls
	Arithmetic	do better with arithmetic tables
are less good at fitting things together and judging how large things are	**Space and Area**	are better at tasks involving fitting things together and accurate judgement of space and area
grow slightly faster	**Growth**	are slightly slower and more uneven in growth
reach puberty younger		reach puberty at later age
will sometimes play with boys	**Play**	will rarely play with girls (more noticeable as they near ten)
tend to be more organised and coordinated		tend towards rough and tumble
tend to perform as well as they can in all subjects	**School**	tend to do better subjects that they have an interest in
tend to evaluate own abilities and performance less realistically		tend to evaluate own abilities and performance more realistically

tend to show more interest in sewing, cooking, art		tend to show more interest in sports, mechanics, science
are more conventional; try harder to fit in	**Socialising**	are not so worried about conforming

There are lots of stereotypes attached to concepts of boy/girl and myths about likenesses and differences. No child totally fits any stereotype.

Research by the Open University[2] showed that there were few differences between boys and girls in the following aspects:
– whether or not the child had a best friend
– whether or not the child preferred to play alone
– whether the child made friends easily
– whether the children could stand up for themselves
– whether they quarrelled with friends
– over fighting with brothers and sisters

The research showed that boys were more likely to come to physical blows with their friends and that parents of boys were more likely to intervene over the friends their child chose.

SECRETS AND PRIVACY

The stories that are favourites for this age-group are often full of codes, secrets, incredible intrigue and adventure. Such choice reflects the children's own interest in the secret and fantastic. Many groups and gangs form their own secret clubs and societies. The rules may be complex and have little meaning for an adult. Some may have adventures that would be questioned if parents guessed what was going on. Most turn out to be relatively safe.

The children should be able to have some secrets. Do get to know the families of your child's friends and the people who live near you, as friends and good neighbours. They will be sure to tell you, without a sense that they are interfering, if they see your child 'up to something'. A neighbour spotted my sister and her friends in a railway tunnel when we were children. The adventure was interrupted and a safer place found. Often children do not realise the dangers they are near and parents, not imagining the real goings on, have not actually forbidden such an unlikely escapade.

Try to offer suggestions for adventure that are within safe limits. Tell your child to avoid games or escapades that she thinks might be dangerous and tell her friends the same, even though they have had no specific instruction from an adult to forbid it.

If you discover that your child and her friends have been into trouble in the neighbourhood, have been damaging property or misusing fireworks, you should probably restrict her time with friends and make her keep to limits much closer to home for a while, until she seems able to be more considerate in her behaviour. Very large numbers of children do get involved in some form of anti-social behaviour, so parents need not be too shocked or too hard on their own children. See the behaviour as a badly directed attempt to find new challenge and to push out to new horizons. Find some more reasonable way to expend creative energy. Perhaps parents and children together can get involved in a physical pastime that is adventurous. Try climbing, abseiling, hill walking, sailing, surf-boarding, all of which are creative challenges to energetic children.

SELF-RELIANCE

Most eleven-year-olds benefit greatly from being expected to care for themselves and for others. The self-respect that is engendered by knowing she can look after herr own needs is important to the child approaching adolescence.

When your child can get herself up in the morning, setting the alarm, getting washed, dressed and ready for breakfast, she can be relied on in making schedules and appointments. Being able to keep her own room tidy and organised results in her privacy being more protected. If a parent has to organise the child into getting up, getting off to school, all her cleaning and tidying, the child is still very dependent and unable to discover herself as a responsible person. All she does still *feels* subject to parents' intrusion and control. There are more likely to be conflicts and arguments as the child struggles for her own sense of identity. When considerable mutual respect is already present, the kind of mutual trust and ability to talk openly that is necessary for teenage years is more readily established.

SEX EDUCATION

Before children reach puberty, both boys and girls should be well prepared for the changes in their own bodies. In contrast with the carefree childhood they have been experiencing, the change, with all its turbulent feelings, may seem monumental to them. Be careful of their feelings.

Find out what books are available and how this subject is taught at school; find ways to complement this. Find general books that show in words and pictures the changes in the body for both sexes from the baby to old age. Look at how the changes happen[3] and talk them over with your child. Consider with the child which picture is most like his or her body now, which is most like Mum and most like Dad. Help your child see herself in the whole picture of life from birth to death. Being male or female is an aspect of that wholeness.

Ensure that the child has a general picture of what is happening to people's bodies, whatever their age, as years pass. Let a boy or girl know that friends are going through the same changes and that boys as well as girls are experiencing change.

For girls find out how books for young adolescents describe menstruation, and how to cope with it. Use the same kinds of description yourself and give her the book to read. Help her understand the changing shape of her body, of developing breasts and body hair.

For boys help him discover the changes that will happen in his body, to the size of his penis and growth of body hair.

Both boys and girls may be extremely sensitive and perhaps embarrassed about themselves and the subject. Children hear all sorts of stories, myths, and fables on the playground and may have some very untrue and destructive ideas. Rate of growth is one of the most worrying. The child whose development is very early or very late may feel a freak, and extremely worried about teasing and hurtful remarks.

Make sure your child has accurate information before his or her body begins to change and reassurance as it does. Make home a safe place for boys and girls, free from teasing or sarcastic remarks. If some chance critical remark is passed among friends the child may then ask a question at home, or even already know that the critic is misinformed.

Only a small number of children find much physical change in themselves by eleven but it is important to have established the trust and openness for conversation and reassurance before a girl has her first period.

Some lone parents find this a very hard subject when dealing with their own children of the opposite sex. It is true that it is hard for a man to reassure a daughter about a period, as he has never experienced one, or about childbirth. It is good for him to be able to talk reassuringly with his daughter, but it can

Friends and Relationships

be helpful for a close female family friend, or the mother of the child's best friend, to have some conversation too. Understanding can come from a parent of either sex, but boys find certain essential reassurance from a man and girls from a woman.

Remember the important thing to note is that knowing themselves and how they grow is the context for a child's learning about the changing body and developing sexual identity. Telling children the 'facts of life' is a minor part of what they should learn about themselves.

QUESTIONS FOR INDIVIDUALS AND GROUPS

1. Remember back to your primary school years and the people who were your friends. What was the name of your best friend, what did she/he look like? How did you become friends? What did you most enjoy together?

In later years, if the friendship changed, what caused the change?

If this person is still a friend of yours, what do you most appreciate about the friendship?

2. What sort of person would you describe yourself as? Are you very similar to your child, or very different? What confusion or empathy comes from this?

3. From what sources did you learn about sex, and the physical changes that would happen to you?

What did you learn from your parents?

What did your school have to say?

What did you hear from peers, both boys and girls?

Would you have preferred to have learned differently? If so how?

Were you confused or embarrassed? Do you remember what caused such feelings to arise?

QUESTIONS FOR GROUPS

1. Listen to one another's memories of childhood friends. From this you may find considerable affirmation of the value of friendship to each person in the group.

2. Read about the friendship between David and Jonathan in I Samuel chapters 18 to 20. From the context, it would seem that David at least was still a teenager, and Jonathan not much

older. However, their friendship is remembered particularly. Go through the story together, noting the qualities that impress you as positive about the friendship, and share your own experiences of these qualities in friendships.

3. What sort of sex education is given in the schools and the church for your children, in addition to what they are taught at home? Borrow some school textbooks and videos of TV lessons to look at together. Let each member of the group say:

which ones they thought were most informative

which ones were most sensitive

which ones were most reflective of Christian standards of morality

which ones they would most/least like their children to see.

Are there constructive comments on the subject of sex education that the group can now offer to the schools and Sunday Schools to which their children belong?

Footnotes
[1] *Living with Children 5 to 10* (Open University 1981)
[2] *Ibid*
[3] *Understanding the Facts of Life*. Susan Meredith (Usborne 1985)

12. ADOLESCENCE

The adolescent child is going through a time of turmoil, a transition from the spontaneity and abandonment of childhood towards a more adult sense of perspective and self-realisation. The term adolescence is relatively modern, for this time of accelerated change in identity, physique and outlook.

There are changes related to growth and physical maturity. There are social and emotional changes that come with the renegotiation of identity in relation to parents and family. Some children are experiencing the first signs and physical changes of puberty at the age of ten or eleven; for others these may come four to five years later. Adolescence and puberty can then describe the stages and changes of children from top of the junior school, in middle school, to the upper years of the comprehensive school.

Parents are able to be of significant help to the adolescent. The child experiences rapid change in his or her body and perceptions, attitudes and feelings. Parents can offer understanding, through appreciating the renegotiation that the child is processing, and stability, through being steady in their love and commitment. Being understanding and able to offer encouragement, being tolerant of anti-social responses and being able to overcome feelings of rejection at a child's choices, are creative and constructive attitudes in parents of this age-group. Such responses are not automatic, nor are they necessarily easy.

Preparing for this time of transition, parents can help themselves by considering themselves and how they respond generally. To those parents who are more emotional, the changes include times of hurt and anger; to those who like order and the regularity of family life the adolescent appears very disruptive and even destructive. For parents who have a close friend to talk to, as well as being able to have affirming conversation with one another, it is easier to cope. Above all it is helpful to realise that young adults of today have to go through these growth processes, to struggle against the patterns of childhood because they must learn to cope in a world of constant change.

A child's upbringing, however good it has been, is insufficient for the future and children must discover the ways and principles involved in being responsible for themselves.

PHYSICAL GROWTH

Girls tend to reach puberty before boys. The changes can be expected as follows:
The girl begins to grow more rapidly, two or three inches in a year.
Her breasts begin to swell.
Pubic hair becomes more visible, darker and thicker.
First period, on average between twelve and thirteen years old.
Breast growth is completed by later teens
Some girls have their first period as early as eleven years old, some not till they are fifteen or sixteen. The paraphernalia of tampons and sanitary towels at first seem cumbersome and discouraging, so make sure she knows how to use them before she needs them. Occasionally a girl finds her period has begun both inconveniently and unexpectedly; be sympathetic and extra sensitive to her feelings. In addition, a girl may suffer from some premenstrual tension/depression. About fifty per

cent of women suffer from considerable pre-menstrual symptoms that are unnecessary, in that treatment is possible. If your daughter is affected with depressions, water retention, moods, aggressive outbursts or other unusual patterns in the days after the middle of her menstrual cycle (up to the onset of the period) encourage her to see the doctor. The WellWoman clinic may be the most helpful.[1]

Maintain a healthy positive approach when you talk to her. A period is not an illness, like having a baby this is a life process.

Talk to your daughter about bras and how to buy one that fits well. Some girls choose to wear no bra, but in many circumstances they may find it more comfortable to wear one. Girls talk among themselves, encourage one another and go shopping together. This may be the most affirming for your daughter.

Keep in mind that both boys and girls mature earlier today than they did twenty years ago, so comparisons with parents' own growing up and teenage years may mislead them.

Boys mature later than girls; to girls they may seem silly and childish. While girls reach the age of being concerned about looks and cleanliness and image in their early teens, boys often seem to be reacting against this till later, to the frustration and concern of many parents.

The following physical changes are happening in adolescent boys:

Testicles begin to develop.
Penis begins to grow and pubic hair becomes apparent.
Voice changes and facial hair develops.
He experiences his first ejaculation (and wet dreams).
Height increases rapidly.

Boys may be particularly worried if such changes happen later than for their peers, they may be discouraged to be still treated as children when more mature looking friends are treated as adults.

A boy may be worried about absence of body hair, the size of his penis, his rate of growth. To be too short is to be at risk of non-acceptance as a man. Male body stereotypes are as strong as those for the female body and boys may be extremely fearful of their own failure to conform to the required image.

Help a boy with his self-image by talking about the stereotypes, talking about acceptable men who do not conform to the 'image'. Help him with his physical questions with reliable and unemotional descriptions of the growing body.

EMOTIONAL CHANGE

With all the emotional change of puberty a young teenager's moods may seem to be one extreme or the other, elated or depressed. This may include times of deep depression, sometimes dragging on for weeks. Its roots are in both physical changes and the teenager's reassessment of her identity. A teenager is no longer comfortable as an extension of her parents, and is struggling inwardly to find who she is for herself. At the same time her changing body is not giving her the positive messages she wants. The growth changes experienced result in a lack of physical co-ordination and an accompanying sense of confusion.

Growing uses energy and the teenager eats more, and needs to sleep more at a stage when she would most like to appear adult, staying up later at night. All these aspects add to the struggle for identity that the young teenager finds as contradictions and tensions within herself.

FINDING IDENTITY

Teenagers are establishing their own identity within the family and in the wider community. They are looking outwards to observe and consider alternative values to those held by their own families. They do this in order to decide for themselves the basic premises by which they want to live. This is not a simple act of rebellion though it may look like one sometimes. They re-evaluate and question in order to discover life values in their own right.

Such a process results in change in the family's life. As the expectations and aspirations of teenagers vary from those of their parents, there are stressful and conflicting positions within the family. It is during these years that the family's ability to listen to one another, to renegotiate previously established positions, and their tolerance are stretched to its fullest.

The pressure of changing identity and the need to know themselves in the wider community can happen with minimal family tension if parents know what is happening, can be tolerant and open to talking, and are able to accept the changes without becoming defensive. Teenage years can be frightening for parents; their protective role made life safe for their children and now the protective boundaries are going through drastic renegotiation. Fathers, often fearing that their daughters are too vulnerable, tend to be very protective. They may fear

Adolescence

their sons are not manly enough, lacking courage and muscle. Mothers are fearful of pushing their children out of the nest before they are able to cope.

Teenagers are emotionally vulnerable. Their need to find their own identity in a wider circle means that other young people or adults may easily hurt or manipulate them. Probably both circumstances happen to most people. Parents may help with occasional questions, 'Are you sure . . . ?' But not directives. They can be sympathetic with their children when they feel discouraged and depressed. When they have been hurt, help pick up the pieces practically and find new openings. The balance between being helpful and being protective is a fine one and varies from person to person and day to day. Parents can be available to offer, but slow to help unless asked.

The work of renegotiating their identity has to be done by the young teenagers themselves; there is little parents can do to help, except to be friends. Many of the normal limits parents impose on their children now have to be seen in a different light. Include teenagers in discussions about appropriate times to be in on Saturday night. Listen to their viewpoints and agree together on the limit. If they fail to keep to their agreement, find out why. Talk about whether the agreement was realistic or what else happened to change things. For example: Make an agreement about the time to come home on Saturday night after a disco. What should they do if plans fall through, and they find themselves unable to get home on time? It would be reasonable for them to phone you and tell you of the change so you are not worried, imagining him or her lying injured in the hospital.

Sometimes a teenager recognises that the person who was going to give her a ride home cannot do so after all. The teenager should know that they can always turn to parents for help. Plans do go wrong, especially when young people are inexperienced at organising themselves and others.

A teenager's plans may be affected by finding that the person with whom she/he made arrangements cannot be trusted. Many young people are sexually harassed. This is the age-group in which there are the greatest numbers of sexual offences against children, and far more of these offences are committed by friends, relatives and acquaintances than by strangers. If a child is unwilling, even for unspoken reasons, the parents should be very cautious about insisting a child take a lift with someone he or she is obviously unwilling to trust. The child may be too ashamed and embarrassed to tell anyone about an incident that has already happened, or fears that hints already made may be taken further.

Friendship is based on mutual give and take, not domineering behaviour and attempts to control. If parents find themselves in a routine of nagging, manipulating or punishing a teenager, they should reconsider their approach. In the transition to adulthood, the young person must be part of agreements and understanding. If parent and teenager cannot talk to each other find a friend to help, or find help from a family counsellor. It is worth the time and energy spent. A breakdown in your relationship now, particularly if this is stormy or violent, can result in your child simply packing his bags and leaving. The friendship the parents would like may never be re-established.

FRIENDSHIP

Teenagers concentrate a great deal of energy on friendships. Family relationships, particularly with parents, are comparatively established and are a support structure on which the young adults depend. The establishment of identity in broader circles is much affirmed by peer friendships.

Socially, teenagers begin to spend time developing romantic and other special relationships among their peergroup. Discos, clubs, and concerts tend to be meeting places for young people as well as entertainment. Such meeting places bring together young people from a variety of places and backgrounds, and their experience in negotiating friendships, being at ease socially, handling conversations with strangers, meeting and accepting new and different people are all stretched.

Initially most young adults feel shy and unable to establish themselves but usually the group of friends and acquaintances with whom they go out, provides enough encouragement and security for them to learn the skills they need socially. So the younger teenagers in a club can be seen whispering to each other, nudging and pushing one another forward with instructions on how to start a conversation.

The acceptance of the group of friends to which most teenagers belong, is an essential part of this socialising process. Only today's teenagers know the subculture sufficiently thoroughly to help one another in its language and mores. Parents belong to another age and culture.

Be tolerant, not critical or cynical, with the ways of teenagers. Just as each generation of younger children has a phase of fearing bad luck if they step on the line between paving stones, so each generation of teenagers has its own valid forms, codes and patterns.

It is fitting in with these patterns that reassures teenagers that they are accepted by their peers. Without the patterns and codes they would lack the messages and assurances of belonging and being acceptable. Each small group of friends reflects fashion trends, ways of speaking, attitudes to music, myths and recollections. Often a small group of girls dress in identical colours and styles.

This group acceptance is far more important to the teenager than parental acceptance of styles. It does not mean that your daughter is ceasing to think for herself, ceasing to be the distinct and creative person that she is potentially. This is a stage at which the signs of belonging are more important than the signs of individuality. By later teens there is again more individuality apparent.

Be encouraging and affirming, look carefully and find ways to affirm your teenager in choices of hairstyle and clothes, not necessarily because the choice suits you, but because you want to affirm the person in her life choices.

EDUCATION

The teenage years are a significant stage in schooling and education. Up till now children have been learning the skills of study, learning how to learn. By the teenage years they are acquiring the learning skills for adult life.

Among school subjects, teenagers begin to learn practical skills of carpentry, metalwork, cooking, housekeeping, needlework. Most schools include some aspects of parenting, but less than necessary for future adult life. Towards the upper years of the school most schools now include some 'Education for Living'. Under this umbrella subject pupils learn many simple and essential tasks of adult working life: opening and using a bank account, making budgets, filling in forms such as those for the Inland Revenue, how to apply for a job, how to vote, and many others.

YOUTH GROUPS

The drive toward being 'grown up', while at the same time expressing themselves in childhood ways is the trademark of the adolescent young teenager. Moods may change from hour to hour, and one minute a teenage boy is playing cops and robbers with the eight-year-olds and minutes later joining an adult conversation in the lounge. Sometimes he is full of creative enthusiasm and minutes later is sleepy and uninterested.

Working on the Children's Programme at Christian conferences, in addition to several years as a teacher and youth leader, I found that the ideal group for the younger teens recognised as many as possible of these attributes. The group had a name that identified it as a 'teens' group rather than a children's group. There were several leaders who were relaxed and friendly, happy to undertake activities, but equally happy to sit around and talk with one or more of the group members. The refreshments were no longer the orange juice and biscuits with which we provided the children's groups, here there were cans of cola, crisps and KitKats for sale. The programme was flexible, having several leaders (both sexes represented). The members were able to be active, playing games, undertaking large projects such as pottery using a kiln they built themselves, sports, serious discussions, or just lazing around doing almost nothing. Invariably there were members who wanted to do nothing, and in making that part of our outline we found that

Adolescence

these young people were able in the relaxed atmosphere to share their sense of frustration, of despair or failure. Many told of their sense of alienation from their parents and lack of a sense that anyone understood or cared how they felt. The adult team leading the group found that listening is the greatest gift, giving relevance and understanding to the child's communication.

Such groups in the church setting provide for the same needs in the adolescent. This is a safe place to be both childish and adult in attitudes and behaviour, without criticism or even comment. The setting, if relaxed and not too tightly programmed can offer a forum for conversation and discussion with adults who are not the parents of the group. Parents can feel confident of their young people being in a group that has an adult feel, but has trusted supervision. The leaders in their acknowledged Christian commitment are not violating the values of the parents and the church. Youth Groups give easy-going social contact, but the integrity of the leaders and the Christian nature of the group provide a level of safety to that contact which is dependable. In developing their programmes groups can include opportunity for supervised adventure and challenge, and for group holidays. The group also contributes to providing young people with a transition time from being children to being adult members of the church, able to take responsibility for themselves and others.

Even if the young teens group is very small it does not mix well with a group for those aged over fourteen, whose life tasks, and approach to life and the church are very different. The older teenagers are concerned about issues that the younger ones find irrelevant and beyond their means to discuss, and the older ones often complain that the younger ones are childish and silly. It is better for both to have their own groups.

QUESTIONS FOR INDIVIDUALS AND GROUPS

1. Remember your own early teens, the feelings and pressures you felt. Did your parents understand you, did you tell them your feelings?
   Who was the person who helped you most at the time?
   What help was the church?
2. How well is your child prepared for puberty and adolescence? Are they prepared for the physical changes in their body? If a girl, is she prepared for menstruation?

Have you and your partner talked over with your child the principles of marriage as the relationship in which sexual intercourse is expressed?

What opportunities does your child have to hear and discuss Christian marriage principles in the church or at school?

Undertake some research to discover the syllabus of the church youth group on the subject of relationships. Look at the church bookstall or the local Christian bookshop for books for young teenagers on relationships and growing up.

QUESTIONS FOR GROUPS

1. Listen to one another's reflections on adolescence as you experienced it.

Having heard everyone, are there any particular ways in which you hope your children have a better time?

List these ways and through discussing these together, see if there are changes that could be made in the life of families, the discussion group or the church, that would help the young teens.

2. Is the whole church aware of the needs of the young teens to have a group of their own, and is the church making suitable leaders available?

Are there ways that this group, having considered aspects of the personal development of young teens, could help the church with young teens?

Footnote
[1] *Once a Month*, Katharina Dalton, Fontana, 1983

13. AUTHORITY

BIBLICAL AUTHORITY

All authority has its source in God, who is the author and creator of all things. To discover authority that is healthy and good in the human context, in society, requires Christians to renew and rediscover the meaning of authority in God.

For those readers who have a particular interest in this aspect it would be recommended that they undertake a theological study of authority. Here, we will only be mentioning a few introductory aspects; readers may wish to look up the passages mentioned and make more detailed notes on the implications of the biblical revelation of God's authority.

Genesis 1:28–31. God blessed the people, male and female made in his image. He gave them dominion (authority) over every living thing that moves on the face of the earth.

Though people subsequently sinned God did not revoke that giving of authority, which was a form of stewardship.

Consider how this relates to authority and the people of the earth. Read the curse on man and woman in Genesis 2:16–19.

Romans 8:18–23,28. The Jews had a word, *Shalom*, which is normally translated 'peace', for which there is no more direct English translation. But the biblical word includes the concept of all things working together in harmony, this is the working together that Paul refers to. For Christians to consider authority it is necessary to see this in the context of *Shalom*. Any Christian exercise of authority will be carried out in broad concern for the harmonious working together for the good of those who are touched by it.

Mark 10:17–22: Matthew 18:1–4; Matthew 20:25–28. Jesus taught and used authority that was neither domineering nor authoritarian. When speaking to the Rich Young Ruler, one of many people who looked to Jesus as authority, Jesus told him what he needed to hear but was not domineering. The exercise of authority in Jesus' own life was both firm and gentle.

The redemption of the world in Jesus brought in a new age for people in their relationship to God, when to give oneself to his authority was no longer to be the endless pursuit of a right relationship through the law. In Ezekiel we read that God will put his Spirit within us and cause us to walk in his statutes and observe his ordinances. With the Spirit authority would find new meaning. Instead of being an external authority against whom people react, the Spirit of God would be within his people, so authority would reflect givenness rather than imposition.

There are, of course, many biblical passages to study and absorb before understanding of authority can be reached. Those mentioned here may introduce readers to a useful search for understanding relevant to raising children.

SOCIETY AND AUTHORITY

There are many social norms that limit what individuals or groups can do. Certain forms of behaviour are acceptable while others are not. The authority that decides and controls such laws is put there by the people to order and stabilise society. That authority is administrated by all sorts of agencies of a democratically chosen government. The police force keeps the populace within the limits of criminal law; social services help keep the limits of reasonable care for children; truancy officers make sure children get the statutory education. Such rules and conventions are there for everyone's care and safety: they protect the interests of the dependent from the interference of the greedy; they settle difficulties at every level, from neighbours quarrelling, to lawsuits between international companies or governments.

There are many opinions about the nature of authority and its administration. Some conclude that 'authoritarian' styles of leadership are 'bad' while others think that such hierarchical leadership is helpful. Voting at General Elections is about choosing the authority the people want. Then too, there are many opinions about how those leaders who are given authority should administrate it, and so voters scan the manifestos to see whose policies most suit them at the time. In general in the western nations, people would rather have democratic forms of government, knowing that 'dictators' work in their own interests and not in ways chosen by society. People want to safeguard against leadership based on megalomania, power seeking, or personal aggrandisement. These are seen to be negative attributes of leadership, an abuse of authority.

In every social group, including the family, there are forms of authority. Parents have a natural responsibility in the authority structures of the family. They are capable of being the leaders; children are not. Just as there are norms of order, safety and security that are expected of national government so there are norms expected of families. Certain forms and ways of exercising that authority are acceptable or tolerable, while others are not. In some situations society accepts corporal punishment, but beyond certain limitations the use of physical force becomes child battering.

Within these imposed boundaries, parents exercise authority in the home and family. On the whole, good parenthood is seen as that which unselfishly cares for and nurtures the children. While children are under the care of parents, they are not owned. Children are people in their own right who, because they are dependent and helpless, need parents to care for their interests on their behalf. Most of what is associated with good government, should also be associated with parenting children, who have no choice, and extreme care taken to avoid the destructive qualities of the dictator. There are many acceptable styles of parenting; some are more authoritarian than others. All parents have their own ways of running the family, of exercising that authority to the best of their ability.

As children grow up, parents have less and less need to be in authority *over* them and more need to establish shared authority. Children become adults and are then peers with their parents, hopefully becoming friends who choose together how to order their life. This is not always an easy changeover. The more authoritarian the family structure, the more likely it is that teenagers will be compelled to leave home in order to have authority in their own lives. 'Dropping out' is a modern phrase to describe the young adults who choose an entirely different form of authority for their own lives, and attempt to escape the authority of both parents and society in general. For some the transition into responsibility is a time of fear for parents and frustration for children and not only are there angry children but angry parents too. If, however, parents can make it possible for young adults within the family to have real authority in their own lives and in the family, there is less pressure to leave to become entirely independent.

FAMILY AUTHORITY

Parents are under the authority of their relationship. In choosing marriage as a partnership, they have chosen to be committed to one another and to live in mutual agreement. Their choice to be married limits them in a variety of ways, for example, to the vows they made in the marriage ceremony to love and honour one another. It is a chosen authority, supported by society in laws and expectations, and it is to the Christian a life-long choice.

In the order and structure of western society today it is increasingly invalid to build family authority around an autocratic model. Previous cultures and societies have done so, normally designating to the 'man of the house' rights of ownership and control over the other members. There is still considerable support for such a pattern, on the grounds that this model is good if used benevolently. The longstanding origins of this lie in male physical strength and tribal structures. These have changed so significantly that the model has become one in which parents are peers and authority is given in ways appropriate to that family. New patterns have been necessary in family decision-making. It is no longer true that the man has the right to control family decisions. There has been a fundamental move towards decision-making by consensus.

This type of change in society and culture must be discussed and assessed in the light of Kingdom principles, not automatically endorsing change as good, but not holding back when, through the Spirit, God is himself working the change.

There are ways of behaving that interrupt decision-making by consensus. Men have maintained control by physical strength, by threat of violence, both in society and in the family. To counteract this, women are quite likely to use subtle forms of manipulation, favours and emotional pressure, like moods. When both of the partners have rights there is neither the need, justification, nor even defence, for any of these patterns. Only if a man has the *right to own* (and thus control) can he be justified in beating his wife into submission. If she has the rights of a person in their relationship she will be respected. If he is not domineering and dictatorial she should not resort to underhand forms of control through favours. This approach to relationships is far more mature and requires far greater sensitivity and understanding from both partners, more love and listening, more respect and care, more give and take.

All this is critical to the life of the family. As the parents together are able to share authority, to cope with one another's opinions and rights in decision-making, are able to come to decisions by consensus, it will be possible for their children to grow into a sense of their own authority without having to withdraw from the family to do so. Those who have grown up in an environment where decisions are taken by mutual consent, have experienced and learned the skills for shared authority.

In the long term, parents always have the *relationship* of mother and father, but the role will change. In primitive societies the roles changed when the up and coming young man could fight for the place of chief, requiring all other men in the family or tribe to be under his authority. In contemporary society people have more right to choose and change that authority, not by a primitive tribal system giving control to the strongest and biggest, but for the good of the community.

UNDER AUTHORITY

The small child is under the authority of her parents, an authority she has not chosen and one which she cannot side-step. Parents are entrusted with the authority for bringing up the child in safety and security. It is their responsibility to see that she grows in a healthy environment, and, acknowledging their authority, society holds them to blame if something goes wrong. There are very specific laws and guidelines to help decide if that authority should be taken away. If a three-year-old child puts her hand in the fire, the parent is held responsible; the parents may be prosecuted for not having a fireguard. Authority may be removed and the child made a ward of court if the parents violate the child, whether actively, in beating or incest, or more passively, in neglect. Once the child reaches eighteen then the parents are deemed to have no authority and the young adult votes, drives, marries as he chooses. The parents guide the child toward responsibly dealing with other authorities and the established patterns of society. The child grows from the complete helplessness of childhood, to take charge of herself and eventually take part in the system of choosing the government that is operated nationally.

Firstly, the child comes to recognise the authority of her parents. The egocentricity of the baby is the first stage, when in her eyes it seems that her cries instruct mother to bring food and she brings it, to pick her up and this happens. She is not being selfish because she is unable to recognise the other person as a person in her own right.

By the time she reaches two years old a child can wait for her needs to be met but still demands that she gets what she wants immediately. It's up to parents to say 'No'. Very often the toddler challenges their authority. They do not allow her to play with the electric plug but a child will go back to it whenever it is taken away. When she realises that her parents are going to limit her, the result may well be temper tantrum. She may be angry, or sad and unsure of herself. But for safety she must be under that authority and held to parents' decisions. Parents must know that when they say 'Stop' the child will not run into the road.

While the exercise of real authority is essential, parents all exercise it differently; some are more insistent on particular forms of behaviour than others.

There are a variety of options over table manners or bedtimes. But it's the parents who decide how insistent to be over such issues. Rules for safety are protected by laws to which parents must adhere. No parents may leave children alone in the house till they are fourteen. However much parents or children disagree, this is not an area that they have choice about. Similarly for smoking, playing with fireworks, driving a car. A responsible parent is exercising authority.

The toddler challenges the parents' right to exercise authority as she would like to be lawless. So when she doesn't have the toy she wants she hits another child to get it. If Mum or Dad try to stop her activity the child may kick them. All are attempts to deny parental authority. Parents have the responsibility for helping their child recognise their authority. Lovingly and caringly, their work includes helping her eventually to take charge of herself and take charge over her own actions. When she is able to be fully in charge of herself in the environment she is allowed to walk to school alone. At ten or eleven, when she recognises the authority of traffic rules, and can co-operate with them, a child can ride a bike on the road alone.

Once the authority of parents is accepted by the child, the work of direction and discipline is much more straightforward. A child meets other authorities with whom he learns progressively to cope. Shopkeepers have authority, and there are limits within which they have authority; customers do not tell the shopkeeper when to open his shop. Customers pay for the goods and are served according to the way of that particular shop. The shopkeeper may change it; customers may not.

Authority

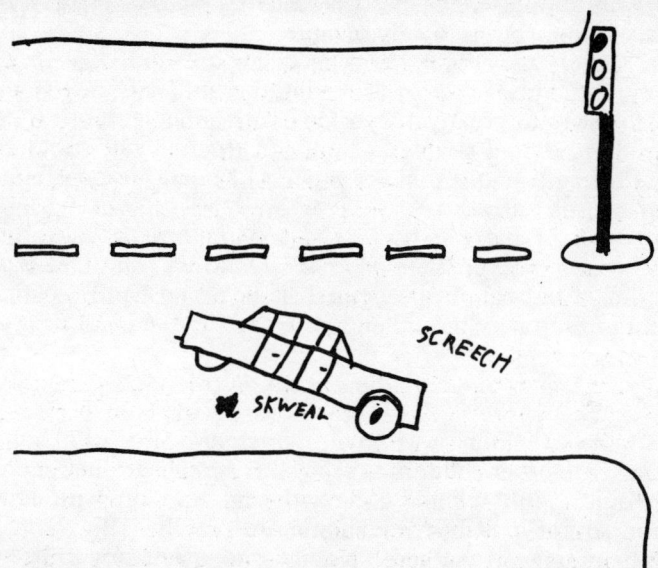

The smooth working of life, its interdependent nature, requires people to recognise such authority. In the story of *Charlie and the Chocolate Factory* by Roald Dahl[2], several greedy demanding children show a number of examples of being unable to accept the authority of others in this way. For example they refused to acknowledge that Mr Wonka had made the rules for his own factory.

Teachers are among the first significant authorities a child meets outside the home. Teaching a large group of children, providing for their learning, organising their work so that their skills and creativity are developed, requires that children and parents accept the authority of the teacher. Through the experience of school the child learns more of what it means to belong interdependently to everyone else. With so many children involved, activities are organised into a defined order; work on certain projects or with particular equipment is co-ordinated. Children come to recognise and work under that authority.

When driving into the town to go shopping, the family becomes aware of traffic wardens, people who are there to encourage the upholding of traffic laws. The local community has authorised them to do the work, for everyone's good.

Through their growing years children experience these and many other forms of authority. The doctor has authority in the field of prescribing medicines that may be unpleasant but we still take them. Some forms of authority a child may hardly notice. Others may limit her where she does not like to be limited. The crucial step of accepting the authority of parents paves the way to creatively working with other authority. As the child grows and is able to look constructively at authority she can become involved in the process of taking responsibility for her chosen authority.

The work of the parents is the foundation for a healthy recognition and acceptance of God's authority, one that is at times defied but cannot be denied, is firm and gentle so that the relationship may be full and rich.

CHALLENGES

One small boy, John, was having great difficulty with doing anything with other children at school. His older brother hadn't settled quickly into school but he had wanted to join with other children so got over his hesitancy more readily. The younger one took a long time. He was a child who was happy to be on his own, preferred to be in control of everything he did and had persistently refused to accept his parents' authority. Having themselves suffered as children from domineering parents, they were unable to bring themselves to insist with this child. When John wanted something he couldn't have, they either distracted him or gave way to his demands, regardless of their own wisdom. In his experience, the first five years had led John to believe he should get everything his way. It was an enormous shock to arrive in school and find that the other children expected give and take in their play and the teacher expected him to join in with the rest of the class. He was much slower than his peers in settling in and beginning to learn the skills of reading and writing.

A young teenager, Suzanne, was going through a very difficult time of depression and fits of crying in despair with herself. As the apple of her parents' eye, she had always been able to manipulate them and was furious if they crossed her. Through her early school years she had few friends – others were put off by her controlling and domineering manner. Now as a teenager she was in despair. She could not hold herself to the things she wanted to do, even homework, as she had never been in charge of herself nor had she let anyone else be. She had always done only what pleased her. The parents could no longer pressurise and manipulate her. More significantly, she

Authority

wanted friendships with boys who soon dropped her when they realised just how selfish she was. She had not respected anyone, not even herself, and would have a great deal of work to do if she was ever to make up for those missed out lessons of early childhood.

Families may have their own problems with external authority. Parents should take responsibility for sorting that out themselves, not leave a child trapped between two contending authorities. If a parent disagrees with a teacher, it's no good complaining and setting the child against the teacher, so they cannot work under her authority. Rather parents should find a resolution to the problem of the difference. A Christian parent may discover that a teacher stated to a class that there is no God; some conversation must be attempted with the school to ask that the teacher recognise the integrity of the family's teaching and not violate it. Each should recognise and support the authority of the other with regard to children. If a teacher finds it necessary to punish a child for misbehaviour the parent may ask for a different form of control but should not expect that a teacher should leave a disruptive or disobedient child to behave wilfully in the classroom. A child will be confused and hurt by conflicting authority. It is up to the parent and teacher to come to some workable resolution about the difference. Resolution only comes with conversation and compromise between the parent and the teacher. For the child's sake it should be attempted.

QUESTIONS FOR INDIVIDUALS AND GROUPS

1. Remember, and make notes on your own experience of authority, with parents, your schools and the church.

    List several particular people who had authority in relation to you, with reasons why you thought they were good. Do you still think so?

    What is your experience of the legal authority, such as the police force, and what is your attitude to it?
2. Undertake a Bible study to discover examples of God's authority in the Old Testament, in the histories, and also in the prophets such as Isaiah who foretold a new age. Consider also the authority of Jesus in the gospels and of the disciples in the epistles.

QUESTIONS FOR GROUPS

1. Tell one another of personal experiences of authority, and attitudes to it.
2. Discover further aspects of authority in the Bible, drawing in the contributions prepared by individuals. Make a summary of your findings.
3. What is the nature of authority in the Christian home today? What does male authority mean, taking note of the statement: 'This type of change in society and culture must be discussed and assessed in the light of Kingdom principles, not automatically endorsing change as good, but not holding back when, through the Spirit, God is himself working the change.'
4. What is the meaning of parental authority in relationship to children who are now adult themselves?

Footnote
[1]*Charlie and the Chocolate Factory*, Roald Dahl, George Allen and Unwin, 1967.

14. ESTABLISHING DISCIPLINE

Discipline is the means of holding oneself or another person to limits, a way of being under control. All externally imposed discipline should be a process during which a child is growing in self-discipline. The parents set these limits for the child, or later the adult sets limits for herself with consideration for her own aims, expectations and the norms of society. A person who is entirely without discipline does exactly what comes to mind at any moment, regardless of her own ambition, values, safety or the rights of others.

Christian discipleship is choosing to follow Christ, a self-discipline.

A baby is entirely without self-discipline, and, limited by her physical abilities and dependence, is disciplined by parents who will both limit her activity and gradually teach her to discipline herself. The child is gradually given more responsibility as it is apparent she is able to make choices about what she does. A child who is able to choose whether to buy sweets now, or to save her money for later, is probably ready to have responsibility for pocket money. The child who, at the moment of receiving money, can only consider how to get to the sweetshop by the fastest possible route, should have more limited access to money. In that she is controlled by her own urgent demand and is not able to consider and then choose, she is lacking the ability to discipline herself.

Ideally, adults have a considerable sense of self-discipline, though it is clear that a person who cannot help but buy chocolate bars even though she is dieting, has difficulty with self-discipline. Criminals who break the law out of choice but are capable of making a different choice are punished with prison sentences, as a deterrent. The psychopath has no control over behaviour and is detained for the protection of others.

The process by which a person is able to discipline herself includes aspects of experience, understanding and self-control. The toddler will have most limits set for her without choice.

She is limited from playing with electricity, saucepans on the stove, from running freely near the road. Eating habits, bedtimes, behaviour patterns, and playspace are established by the parents on the child's behalf. In sixteen years she is transformed into a person who can choose her own eating habits, plan schedules, order her work life, get up in the morning at a prescribed time and be a responsible member of the family, perhaps choosing her marriage partner.

This ability to work or play within limits develops gradually and intentionally. Parents talk very little about the limits they will set for their child. If they are fairly like-minded and easy going this will work. Each of them will raise questions if they cannot agree on any specific limit when it comes up in their daily circumstances.

There are, however, two values in talking over the kinds of limits you plan to set. If either or both of you grew up with parents who held an extreme discipline, either very strict or very lax, you could easily fall into two extremes yourselves, either living out a set of limits that go as far as possible from what your parents did, out of reaction against them, or simply repeating the ones your parents set, out of your ingrained fear. Either way, if your child oversteps your limits or questions them you may be unable to respond except with a strong emotional reaction. You may well be unable to offer a considered answer or a compromise. Only through reflection on why and how limits are chosen and imposed will your child benefit from a balanced discipline rather than a legalistic or reactionary system.

The second value is in reducing the number of situations in which you as parents are in conflict or contradict one another. Consider the following charts, filling in your own ideas, and reasons where you know them. Perhaps your spouse can also be persuaded to look at them and say where he or she disagrees with you.

RESPECT AND CARE FOR SELF

Who sets the limit? (Beside each statement write 'child' or 'parents' as it fits your child's life.)

Sets time for bed:

Gets the child in bed on time:

Sets time to get up:

Establishing Discipline 143

Wakens her:

Sets time to go to school:

Gets her ready to leave the house:

Decides how pocket money is spent:

Decides when pocket money is spent:

Dresses child:

Decides when to get dressed:

Chooses clothes for the day:

Chooses clothes in the shop:

Decides how to use spare time:

Decides on clubs:

Chooses friends:

Chooses hairstyle:

Buys shoes:

Decides what to eat:

Decides when to be clean and tidy:

RESPECT FOR OTHERS

Is your child able to show respect?

To play with other children without hitting them?

To ask other children for a toy and take 'no' for an answer?

To express sorrow when she has hurt someone?

To give gifts of her own choice?

To share, by her own choice?

To leave things alone that don't belong to her or are not to be played with?

To treat carefully what is fragile?

To ask before taking something that is not hers?

To know what she *can* take without asking?

To pick up her own toys without supervision?

To help consistently with family chores?

To undertake a task without supervision?

To do homework without reminders?

To practise musical instruments without reminder?

To change their own schedule if someone calls in and plans are disrupted?

These statements are not comprehensive, but illustrate a progression in the ways a child takes responsibility. If she has the skill to do a task, but if not supervised will leave it undone, the child is not disciplining herself and the parent must be the source of discipline. Some of the examples involve other people, the child's friends. If for example the child has not yet reached the stage of being able to ask for what she wants without hurting the friend, play should be supervised. In going through the list look again and decide what your child ought to be able to do now and what you think should be left till later.

Establishing Discipline

LIMITS REFLECTING PARENTS' VALUES

Consider the following list of table manners. For each category, should this begin now, in the near future, sometime in the more distant future, or don't you mind when? Put a tick in the column representing your reponse.

	Begin now	Next few months	Sometime in the future	Unimportant
Drink without slurping				
Use knife and fork				
Say 'please' when asking				
Stop 'dunking' biscuits				
Use a napkin				
Use a hanky, not sniff				
Say 'thankyou'				
Wait for others to finish before leaving table				
Wait for others before beginning to eat				
Eat everything on plate				
Not grumble if there's food on the plate she doesn't like				
Stop talking with a full mouth				

Often these kinds of limits cause great concern for parents and differing opinions can result in considerable argument. Remember that neither of you is right or wrong. The chances are that both of you have the same concerns at heart and your backgrounds will determine which particular manners you are most concerned about. Parents can be very upset about minor issues as their whole background and chosen standards seem to be challenged by the spouse's different viewpoint.

A child's co-ordination develops slowly over the years. Do not try to impose values that she is not yet physically able to manage. Do not confuse lack of skill with disobedience. Some children may use their fingers while eating because the fork is as yet too unmanageable. Let her go back to using a spoon. She will want to grow to using the same as everyone else as fast as she can, so let her grow at her own pace.

TRAINING FOR SAFETY

While table manners are a matter of personal opinion, limits set for the child's safety are not at all optional. The setting and holding of such limits is entirely the parents, responsibility. Liquids such as bleach, cleaning materials and spray cans must be stored away from the child's reach; they cannot be left where an inquisitive or disobedient child might get to them. Similarly, tools and any 'dangerous' equipment must be placed out of the child's reach. Medicine cupboards should be high up, out of reach, and locked. No medicines should be left around even in safety containers. The most simple adult medicines can have a lethal effect on a child. Until a child is old enough to be entirely obedient over the use of any medicine she should not go to the medicine cupboard for anything. Parents should supervise all medication for children under twelve as the child may not appreciate and respect the reasons for the great care that is taken.[1]

Kitchen knives and sharp tools should be introduced carefully so a child can learn their proper use with the least possible risk. A three-year-old may be able to learn to slice food with a serrated knife which cuts the food but not the fingers. Smooth bladed knives should be kept till later on. There are many kinds of round-ended scissors that cut well and are suitable for a child under school age. These are sharp enough to cut the paper but not sharp enough to damage the fingers. Pointed scissors are alright once a child is reaching the top of infant school. Children of ten and eleven can use a craft knife only if

Establishing Discipline

supervised and the same for using razor style cutters or extremely sharp stainless steel scissors. A child under this age does not realise how easily she could cut her hand but by eleven she can learn how to hold things safely while supervised.

There are varying opinions about when children can cross the road safely. Children up to the age of seven are unpredictable; they may easily forget to look before stepping off the kerb. However good their memory is normally, they may be momentarily distracted by a conversation with a friend. If there is a crossing patrol outside the school, your child may manage without parental supervision. After seven the parents can tell whether their child is yet ready for such responsibility alone, by watching how she copes when with them.

There is no law about when a child may ride a bike on the road alone. Until eleven or twelve a child cannot appreciate the strength, speed, and movements of other vehicles and make allowances for them. She must know both the rules of the road and the necessity of keeping to them. The Police 'Cycle Proficiency Test'[2] is a good way of measuring your child's ability to manage on the road and whether you should allow her to go alone. Until a child reaches that stage, take the opportunity of riding a bike alongside her so she can learn from your road safety standards.

An obvious limit for safety's sake is that a child should know from toddler days never to get into someone's car without specific instruction from Mum or Dad. It's good to explain to a child that if anyone invites them to go for a car ride, whether a stranger or a close friend, she should first go in and check with a parent that this is alright, regardless of how well she knows the person. This way parents can keep check on what happens, and avoid fearing the worst when an otherwise perfectly safe trip has been undertaken.

Occasionally a child has been in the habit of visiting neighbours without parents being aware of where she is and there have been tragic results. You may keep check on your child, by asking her to always let you know where she is playing and that she must return to tell you if she want to go somewhere else.

None of these 'absolute' rules is a violation of a child's free choice but are necessary disciplines to protect her. Many skills tackled too soon could endanger the child. Often there are consequences that an adult can foresee that a child could not.

COMMUNICATION

Communicating the limits parents wish to set for a child can often be more difficult than deciding in principle that a limit should be set. There are three kinds of limits to set for children: limits for safety are the clearest; other limits reflect daily routine for the child; finally there are the limits that reflect preferences and personal values, such as table manners.

Fill in the following chart, thinking of the limits you set for your own child. Put in an S if the rule is for safety. Put in an R for ones that reflect essential routines. Fill in a P for preference or personal value. What is your feeling when you set this limit: guilt, frustration, relief, fear?

	Limits I set Yes or No	Why? S, R or P	Feeling eg. afraid
Running into the road			
Speak to stranger			
Use matches			
Go off to play without telling me where			
Play with undesirable children			
Dressing up against the cold			
Wear wellingtons in rain			
Go to bed when told			
Stay up late when he or she asks			
Sweets only on Saturday			
Sweets when the child asks			
Eat up all her food			
Be at school on time			
Choose whether to be in Brownies or Cubs/music lessons			
Choose what to play with			

Establishing Discipline

Put toys away

Choose her own clothes
in the shop

Many of these examples will be instructions that are so obvious you never think about them. Others, perhaps only a few, would be ones against which you have written a strong feeling but are unsure whether to insist or not. This is a personal value, should you or should you not impose it? Instructions that reflect personal values are the ones that may result in the most discrepancy, therefore the most conversation, between parents. One parent may be more cautious, for example, in deciding how high up the tree a child is allowed to climb.

What happens when you are unsure or even feel guilty about the rules you set? In any instruction you give on that particular limit, your child will hear two messages: your words and your tone. One message says do this, while the other message says you might not have to. Which does the child relate to? Usually the second. The parent finds himself being challenged about the child's obedience to the limit that he has been least sure about setting. It will be no help arguing with the child – she will not know how to sort out or explain the two messages she has received. Nor is it reasonable to punish her severely for disobedience. The most helpful course of action would be for the parents to sit down, without the child present, and talk through their feelings about that particular rule, talk over reasons why the child should or should not stay within that limit, and make a decision about what they will hold to in the future. This process will enable them to give one clear message, while resolving the feeling of guilt.

Failing to resolve the double message and confused feelings in the parent can also result in parent and child trying to manipulate one another. Consider the check-out at the supermarket and the rack of sweets shoppers have to pass. The parent doesn't want to buy any more sweets today. The child sees a favourite and asks for it. Dad says 'No' but the child becomes more insistent and whines. Irritated, Dad answers angrily only to realise other shoppers are watching. He's embarrassed and becomes unsure. The child begins to cry and a tantrum may ensue so Dad is sorely tempted to give in. What happens? Will he think 'Oh well, what's all the fuss about a bag of sweets anyway' and buy it? Will he smack the child angrily or withdraw into a bad mood? Whenever a child senses the parent is hesitant in saying 'No' to something for which they ask, they will continue to try for 'Yes'. If they find that pressure results in 'Yes' they will use the same tactic again and again. The only solution is for the parent's first answer on such an issue to be the one to which he sticks.

Do not get trapped into a pattern of punishing a child who keeps asking for the same thing. If the child at the check-out had known that 'No' meant she wasn't going to get sweets, she would not have gone on and on. A child who repeatedly asks has experienced that manipulation and pressure may well get her what she wants. This is a problem of the parent's indecision, not the child's disobedience. The meaning of 'No', like the meaning of other words, is learned through experience. It's the parents' problem if the child has learned that 'No' means 'You'll have to put on a good show before you get what you want'. The meaning of 'No' should be established clearly with a child by the time they are eighteen months old. At that stage the child may get very angry because parents limit them, but to establish it at this age will make future discipline more straightforward.

This is to carry the biblical injunction to let our 'yes' *be* yes and our 'no' *be* no, into our nurture of children.

When instructions are being given to a child, say clearly what is expected, and let the child know by experience, that the parent is going to require this. Be consistent with the words, the tone and the actions. If you require a child to stop something be sure that when she does it again you are going to stop her. If they pour water over the side of the bath and you tell her to stop but the action is repeated, stop the child, either by taking her out of the bath, or taking away the toy with which she pours water.

Just as 'yes' and 'no' should be straightforward so should all instructions, then the child can behave responsibly within clear cut limits. It is very confusing to a child for instructions to be given as questions that appear to give choice. 'Would you like to wash up for me?' It would seem very reasonable for the child to say 'No', as she would if the question were 'Would you like another helping of pudding?' It is not impolite to make instructions clear and direct: 'It is time for you to clean your room.'

Establishing Discipline

DISOBEDIENCE

Deciding on a relevant course of action requires consideration on the reasons for disobedience, or the action the parent takes may well not have the desired effect.

At just over a year old the child is learning the meaning of 'No'. She may learn it in some settings but not readily apply it to others. It is time to have patience about repeatedly stopping an activity while saying 'No', in many different contexts. Being angry, aggressive or overforceful on the parent's part will make it harder for the child to understand the meaning; she may merely become afraid of the angry reaction without recognising the lesson the parent wants to communicate. Above all be gentle and patient.

In early stages of discipline a child may be challenging the parents' right to set the limits. Every child will do this in her own way: she may hear the instruction and, looking very deliberately at the parent, will simply go on doing just as she intended before she was interrupted. The child should be required to obey. Be gentle and patient, this is a normal and healthy stage that a child will grow through. The parents' responsibility is simply to be in charge. Don't be afraid, or overly aggressive. Being in charge can be established very quietly.

As the years go by a child who recognises her parents' authority will, on the whole, be reasonable and straightforward to discipline. However, every child at times deliberately or wilfully disobeys instructions. There may be all sorts of reasons why a child does this: if possible find out why. Occasionally the reasons will be valid, and the child affirmed for breaking a rule set. More often the child will not have a good reason for her disobedience.

Using the messages of chapter two tell your child that you are disappointed, you know she could do better. Repeat your reasons for the rule and ask if she knows that she is to keep it in the future. He or she may say that the rule is irrelevant now. Listen carefully and consider what your child says and change your rule if she is right.

On the occasions that parents find it necessary to redirect their child's behaviour, give an affirming message for the desired behaviour. Assure the child that you know she can do better, 'I am disappointed. I know you can do better than this. Please have another go at cleaning.' When she has finished tell her how you appreciate what she has done, 'I like the way you cleaned your room, it looks good.'

A child may be disobedient through inability to keep to a set instruction or limit. What parents are asking may be too difficult for a child of that age. Small children cannot sit still for very long, nor can they stop crying when told. It would be wrong to punish a child for not being still and quiet in an adult gathering. Instead, the parent should find alternative ways to bring the child into the setting. If your church services are very adult in their form and content, bring your child in for part only or give her a colouring book and crayons so she may quietly entertain herself. You may wish to find ways to change the service so that children may participate and do not become restless.

Since children skip, jump, roll, and run spontaneously, reconcile yourself to having regularly to ask your child not to run in the house or make too much noise. People get more docile as they get older, as well as more conscious of others' sensitivity to noise. A hyperactive child cannot be still; look for a solution other than punishment. An insecure child cannot help clinging to a parent. Make sure that parents are not trying to get a child to do what is physically or emotionally impossible.

Particularly where there are several children in a family the younger ones may consider it unjust that the rules which apply to them are more restrictive, such as being unable to take out a bike like the older ones. Those older will resent having more chores or responsibilities than younger ones. Every child is in her own growth pattern and the stages will be achieved at varying ages. The rules for one may be different than for the others. A particularly 'dreamy' child may not be allowed on the road with a bike as early as the one who is very conscious of what goes on around her. It is just and reasonable to fit limits and instructions to a particular child's growth. Console and affirm, but don't allow her to do what you know to be unwise, even if she says you are being unfair.

Limits and restrictions change as a child grows. She reaches a level of skill that enables her to tackle a task unsupervised. Talk about such changes so the child understands why and when parents have changed the limit. Then she will be able to raise questions about other limits and talk over the reasons for them. 'Dad, would you let me catch the bus with Susan, without you or Mum? I know I can manage alright; I know what to do.' For their own satisfaction parents may want to re-check the child knows what to do. If in doubt whether she is too

Establishing Discipline

young, ask parents with children of the same age, who can give a guideline.

Once children are above the age of challenging your authority very strongly, more than two or three years old, they may reasonably question their parents' position. If it is possible that the rules set are too restrictive or it is time for change, the child should know *how* to question them. If the child has grown beyond old rules and is not allowed to ask about changes, she will rebel or disobey when out of sight. It is much better to talk openly and agree to change now or encourage the child to ask again in a few weeks. In the meantime, find out details and reassess the position; then when parent and child talk together, the parent will have more idea than just a feeling about whether to hold to or change the rule.

In the parent and child relationship there are some areas of decision that are entirely the responsibility of the parents. Some are for parents and child to decide together, while others the child can decide for herself. There is a flow of more areas of decision-making becoming the child's responsibility and less belonging to the parents alone. The time for such changes in who makes the rules can reasonably be raised by parent or child. As much as possible, do not reverse the process and take back the responsibility except in extreme circumstances.

When parents are in the wrong, whether by mistake or intentionally, the child is right to disobey (or to disobey another adult in authority). Realise that for a child's safety she must know there are situations in which she is right to disobey. If parents have set the child a task which she knows she is unable to do safely, such as operating a cooker or looking after a younger child, she is right to say 'No'. Many children who are violated by members of the family, relatives or friends, have not realised they are right to say 'No' to particular adult behaviour. There is now more teaching in schools and other institutions that encourages a child to know that she has the right to stop anyone touching her body in a way that she does not want. Teach your child that she *can* say 'No' on some occasions.

Parents who are wrong should tell a child they are sorry, explaining their error and why it was wrong. Assure your child you will not do it again. If the error resulted in physical or emotional damage, for example if she was interfered with sexually, seek professional help immediately. Trying to keep this a secret causes further emotional and social damage.

Some adventurous parents want their children to tackle activities of which the child is afraid. It doesn't help to force her otherwise this will create more problems; rather see if you can help resolve the fear or leave the child to grow beyond it herself. Parents can be so embarrassed or ashamed of their child's timidity that they over-react cruelly. Boys are condemned as sissies or as 'girls!' when they are afraid. Fear is neither masculine nor feminine nor is overcoming it helped by destructive criticism. This will annihilate self-respect and respect for a parent.

Some children exhibit particular behaviour that reflects inner turmoil. Stealing, lying, excessive shyness, violence, and fetishes may be signs of problems. In any of these cases a person who works professionally with children will be able to help parents discover if the child will simply grow out of the behaviour or if she is in need of therapy. In such situations, again, punishment is likely to create more problems than it solves.

TANTRUMS

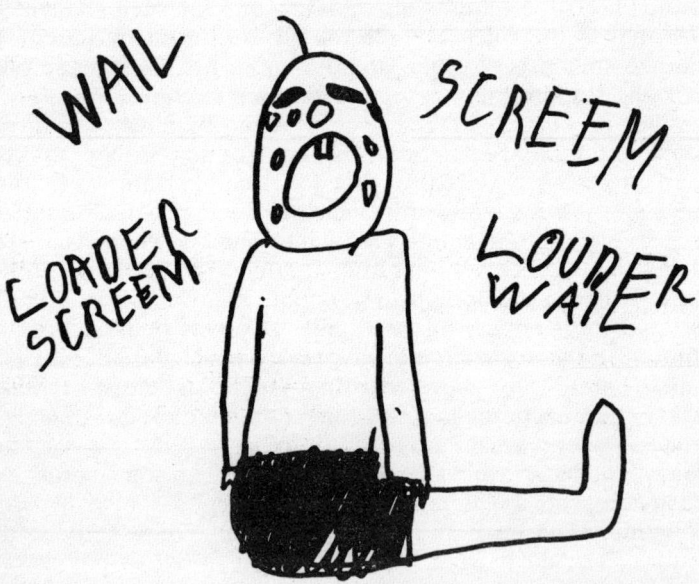

Meeting a limit that restricts a person's desired activity can result in the most creative behaviour. The explorer meeting a crevasse across his intended route will seek to build a bridge or circuit the problem. In sport people are always trying to push beyond their previous best to beat the unbeaten challenge, to defy the odds that seem to be impossible. Florence Nightingale, frustrated by the inadequacy of the old system, established a new style of nursing in the face of much opposition. Many of the numerous inventions in history are the result of creative solutions at the point of someone's frustration. It comes as no surprise that a child who finds opposition to an intended activity will be both extremely frustrated and try to find ways around the limit.

It used to be said that the child's strong will should be broken. But if she is to retain a creative approach to the problems of life there must be another solution. A docile child with a broken will has no resource to overcome the natural problems in life, to achieve new horizons of invention, exploration or attainment. Throughout the world people whose will has aggressively been broken exhibit an inhuman lack of creativity and drive, an inability to protect themselves and a passive acceptance of deprivation and cruelty.

A tantrum, most common in two-year-olds, is an extreme expression of *uncontrolled* frustration and anger. A child realises that her parents are saying 'No' and intend to stick to their decision. The child may be consumed with rage, her screams drown all other voices; she hold her breath till she goes go blue and may throw herself on the floor. It's very dramatic though very normal. No aggressive response is necessary from the parents. They should simply continue to say 'No' if the child tries to repeat the activity. The child may repeat the tantrum, but as long as parents hold peacefully and calmly to their limit he or she will get over it quite quickly. The parents are communicating to the child that they are in authority and have placed a limit.

Parents may be tempted to respond to the child out of their own frustration and rage. Beating and shouting will not help; if the parent allows himself to express rage violently and uncontrolledly against the child, she will in turn be violent. If the tantrum irritates and frustrates the parent, pick up the screaming child and put her in another room telling her that they can come back when they have stopped screaming. That way the parent can take the time to recover from his own response without hurting the child.

Some tantrums are the result of frustration in communication. A child is unable to say what she wants to her parent and finally screams with frustration. She needs sympathy and an opportunity to talk so she knows she can communicate as she wants.

When a child is frustrated by her own lack of skill in a task help him or her break down the task to what she can tackle successfully. Avoid taking over; help a child face new challenges, creatively, looking for a way that she can solve her difficulties.

Some children have more tantrums and carry on longer than others.

Ensure that you are not rewarding the behaviour by giving in, as in the example of the tantrum in the supermarket.

Rage is better expressed than repressed, but don't allow a child to hurt herself or another person when she is angry. If a parent picks up an angry child who then hits out, control her actions, holding her hands carefully. Explain that you will not let her hurt you or anyone else. Similarly, do not allow a child to smash nearby items. Do not reject the child but stay with her till she recovers. Cuddle her and reassure her. With a child who is three years or more, you may also wish to talk over what happened enough for her to know you love her and want to help with her frustration. Tell the child again that she must not hurt herself or you. Tell her that the limit you have set is necessary and that you are sorry she feels so badly about it.

Tantrums are a creative and normal stage on the path toward maturity in expressing feelings and reactions. Rage should be expressed but through creative outlets; in a tantrum a child has no regard for her own safety or the safety and concerns of others. Uncontrolled rage results in violence and aggression that hurts people without necessarily changing the circumstances that caused in the outburst. A sensitive and affirming response from parents takes the child beyond the frustration of tantrums to creative expressions of feeling in more controlled forms.

SELF-DISCIPLINE

The aim in discipline is to enable the growing child to become more and more responsible for her own behaviour. When she is very tiny it may be necessary not only to tell a child that she may not touch a breakable object, but to remove it from her reach. Before long it will help if she chooses to keep within the limits themselves. If she plays with an electric plug and parents tell her to stop, she should do that without having to be removed forcibly.

Establishing Discipline

Three-year-olds can usually recognise consequences, and all children are able to do so by the time they start school. When three-year-olds play with others you will always find some who so much want their own way that they will hit or bite other children. 'Joanne, when you are ready to play without hurting the other children I will let you play with them again. Tell me when you are ready to do that. Till then, sit over here by me.' Ask her occasionally if she is ready to play yet. Some children take longer than others but the limit helps them choose to play more caringly.

A friend's two boys were fighting over a cushion which each wanted to sit on during their favourite programme. 'I'm switching the television off until you both come to tell me you have decided what to do about the cushion and can tell me that you won't fight with each other while you watch.' As a principle, the parent is saying 'If you do this activity, then I will take this action. You choose.' Some children may choose to miss play for a long time or even to miss their favourite programme, but very few young children will make negative choices for long. Older children, who have previously found ways to manipulate parents' instructions and are being faced with a new approach, will take longer.

The early stages of helping a child towards self-discipline and making choices that respect others, may seem tedious. Personal freedom, and freedom of choice, are set in the context of healthy relationships to others. The child becomes an adult in mutually caring and respecting relationships, able to express herself without violating others, able to accept the limitations that come from living in a family and community with others.

QUESTIONS FOR INDIVIDUALS AND GROUPS

1. Go back through the list of 'manners' and tick the ones you are sure you always keep and put a cross by those you don't keep to. Are you expecting your child to do what you don't?
2. Make notes of any questions and thoughts you have about discipline, whether about your own children or general principles. Talk these over with your spouse, or take them to the group discussion.
3. Reflect on your childhood experience. In what ways were the family members corrected? Were compromises made? Looking back do you think the discipline was reasonable or are there changes you would make?

QUESTIONS FOR GROUPS

1. The many aspects of disciplining children raise more questions and reflections than any other topic related to their nurture.

Give time for each group member to share from her own experience as a child.

Are group members attempting to do differently with their own children because of their own past responses to discipline? In what ways?

2. Paul makes a small but significant comment on children in Ephesians 6:4. Why do you think Paul made this point for the Ephesians? What do you as a group think this instruction means for you today?

3. Are there particular limits related to areas of 'personal' preference, such as manners, that the group believes Christian parents should hold?

4. Are there any circumstances in which the group would allow violence from a child, or is this always to be forbidden?

Footnotes

[1] Do not leave strong cleaning agents where a small child can reach them. They may taste them or get them in their eyes. If either of these should happen GET TO A HOSPITAL IMMEDIATELY, TAKING THE OFFENDING CONTAINER WITH YOU. Don't take the risk of waiting; some cleansers are corrosive and by the time there are symptoms, precious time has been lost and permanent damage done.

Similar action should be taken if a child takes medicine, either an overdose of their own medicine or an adult's medicines. Take them to a hospital immediately, *with* the medicine container. DO NOT WAIT FOR ADVERSE SIGNS, GO IMMEDIATELY.

Do not leave contraceptive pills on the bedside table or easily available in the kitchen. These too are harmful to children.

It may not be necessary to include such information here, but I do so because it is possible that though some of these instructions would seem obvious, parents do turn up at a hospital without a sample of the offending item which only causes delay in treatment. Hence a reiteration of basic safety instructions.

[2] Primary Schools or the local Police Station will be able to give you details of local Cycle Proficiency training. This is usually arranged between the school and the local Police when children are in the top year of junior school.

15. CORRECTION OR PUNISHMENT

On the occasions that parents find their intervention is required in response to their child's disobedience, correction is more important than punishment. All methods of correction must be orientated towards changed behaviour; punishment may not stop the child doing the same again. Forms of correction that break a child's will, her sense of being a good person, a lovable person or of being one capable of behaving well, should not be used.

SPANKING

Spanking is a severe form of correction, both frightening and humiliating for the child. Being spanked can result in resentment and withdrawal. It always hurts, and the child who shows no reaction is fighting to hide how deeply she is hurt, and his or her sense of violation may damage an adult and child relationship. Other forms of correction are as effective as spanking without the accompanying dangers. I recognise however that some parents may want to use spanking as a method for correcting their children, though I would recommend that even then they only use it on very rare occasions.

Look again at the section on disobedience in chapter fourteen on page 151. There are several situations shown in which a child may be disobedient. In only one circumstance would spanking be appropriate: that is for wilful disobedience, when the child has *consciously* decided; he set out to do what you have clearly forbidden, with no acceptable reason. Did the child remember you telling her not to ride her bike outside the gate? If she did and chose to ignore you because she wanted to play outside by the road, then they have been disobedient. She could have come in to you and asked you to change your instruction, but rather than risk hearing you again deny what she wanted, she went ahead. This is consciously being disobedient.

Consequences
In the story of Esther, Mordecai gave a clear consequences message to Esther when she was queen. When the death of all Jews was decreed, Esther was unsure about helping their plight. But Mordecai told her that *if* she kept quiet *then* the result would be that her house would perish. Read the full story in the book of Esther; this incident is in chapter eight.

Whenever a parent is correcting a child's activity, and change is required, use a 'consequences' message. '*If* you do that *then* I will spank you.' If the child then disobeys you follow through and spank him. Do not spank without the consequences message. Similarly if the child is told she will be spanked the parent must keep her word to the child and do it. Do not save the spanking till later. An effective spank is a sharp slap or two on a child's naked upper legs or his bottom. This will sting your hand and the child and is enough of a shock while causing the least possible physical effect.

NEVER use a stick, a shoe or other implement.

NEVER strike any other part of the body, such as the trunk or the head.

NEVER use any other violent or physical punishment.

Stay with the child and comfort her affectionately.

NEVER reject the child; hold her close until she has fully recovered from her tears and is aware of your love. Do not leave her to run off and cry on her own. Reassurance is always essential.

NEVER spank a baby and be very cautious about spanking a toddler. It is too easy for her to misunderstand what is meant both by the instruction and by the spanking. Teach a toddler the basics of 'No', and of coming when she is called, by affirming her for the times they does and is obedient.

An angry parent must **NEVER** punish with physical force. The child equates the anger with the spanking and rather than correcting behaviour, she is more likely to be on the lookout for when Mum is angry. If a parent is angry when she spanks, she rejects the child emotionally and this is more harmful than if the child is left unspanked. The angry parent who is giving way to uncontrolled rage is battering the child as an expression of her own feelings, striking out in an adult tantrum.

Find a way to take charge of your own feelings if your child's activity has resulted in your being angry. Leave the room for

Correction or Punishment

a while, send the child to her own room, talk to a friend, or take any other break that will enable you to get some perspective on the situation and look for a way to help your child.

If parents are spanking their child frequently, that is more than once in every few months for children up to the age of five, and almost never for a seven-year-old and older, something has gone wrong in the discipline/self-discipline process. Perhaps parents are being inconsistent in some way or a family pattern is causing the child to be repeatedly disobedient. Seek help from a social worker or, for a young child, the Health Visitor. Talk over the child's behaviour and see if a new perspective can be found.

If you have any thought that you may be punishing your child too severely, however hard they may tax your resources, for their sake and yours, find professional help. Contact a doctor, social worker, teacher, or organisation that offers to support parents under stress.[1]

If spanking children to control their behaviour is not advisable then other methods must be found, that are effective in achieving parents' aims and less damaging in their side-effects.

CONSTRUCTIVE CORRECTION

Many methods for correcting children are recommended by contemporary experts on child development. All work to a considerable extent, but in the end parents will assess which approaches work for them and their children, with consideration to personality and life values.

Parental Approval[2]

A baby's primary relationship with her mother is one of affection, love and warmth. The baby's first smiles are for her. She begins to look for and depend on her mother's love and wants her to be close by. The baby will miss her quite deeply if she is in hospital and her development will suffer if separated from her for long.

When the young child's mother disapproves of her actions, she feels she has withdrawn from her and looks for her return. At first she may cry, hoping in that way to get her attention and bring her back, just as she does when she needs food. Disapproval may be expressed in body language without words, in a tone, a posture, a facial expression. In her discomfort, the baby wants to return to the previous warmth. As soon as she is able to pick up the link between her own action and her mother's disapproval she wants to change her actions.

As other adults the child loves also show disapproval, they will respond similarly and an inner drive to respond and act according to adult expectations will be under way. She knows that to step out of line with an adult's expectations takes her outside the warmth; an unpleasant experience.

To teenagers going through the process of assessing and deciding their own standards for life, the parental disapproval will still be an important factor, as the parent's values and expectations and love are stabilising factors in their changing world.

In this socialising process 'through a caring adult . . . the child learns to care.'[3] The way in which the adult relates and cares for the child, for other people, for other creatures and the world around, will influence how the child learns what is expected of her. Since the adult will show signs of disapproval, maybe as little as a frown, at the child's carelessness, the child's inner drive will make her conform more and more to the adult's model.

Eventually a child will internalise standards presented by parents. She will have become self-disciplined – she feels guilty if she behaves outside those norms.

Correction which is authoritarian, domineering, which lays down sets of legalistic rules – 'I said it, so you've got to do it!' – without conversation and subsequent understanding, will always be an externally imposed authority against which to fight. Such imposed rules 'require punishment, fear and external control'[4] to limit the child's behaviour. Both the teenager and the adult will rebel – they will learn to beat the system and be proud when they manage to.

It is constructive to develop a consistent and loving approach to discipline, with conversation and tolerance that promote understanding and self-discipline. The process from parent-only decisions toward child-only decisions will be facilitated, along with interdependence and mutual care.

Time Out

According to the child's age and ability, different ways are used to develop the ability to care and co-operate. Just as a child wants a mother's love and affection, she will enjoy family times together. From toddler-age upwards exclude the child from the group when she persists with actions that are inappropriate and against the parents' instruction. If you wish to stop her misbehaving at the table take her out of the room until she realises she cannot rejoin everyone unless she changes her behaviour. If a child won't eat her food, make sure that this is not just a stage when she is not very hungry. If, however, it is obvious she is refusing to eat because she likes the negative attention this brings, or refuses a main course but screams for pudding, then refuse the child the right to choose. Allow no snacks between meals, so she will be hungry when she comes to the table. Do not use sweets and puddings as a bribe ('If you eat this up I have a wonderful pudding for you') or she will crave sweet things as a sign of affection. But in a quiet, matter of fact way (and despite any wailing) give no pudding if she does not eat the main course.

One small boy was always making a fuss in church, especially during times of quiet, and his mother was almost ready to abandon going to church altogether. Then a friend, who knew the child well, carried him outside everytime he made a fuss, telling him they would return when he was ready to be quiet with everyone else. He wanted to get back with his family and soon learned more reasonable behaviour. In just the same way a child may be taken away from the table if she misbehaves during a meal or other family activity. Do not provide a pleasant and distracting activity while out of the room; let the company of the rest of the family be the attraction that draws her into the behaviour parents want.

Privileges
By the time a child reaches school age she may be corrected through a loss of privilege that is directly related to a favourite activity. Earlier there was reference to the boys who lost their TV programme through fighting for a cushion. The child who through carelessness breaks a window with his football may lose pocket money to help repair the damage. A child who keeps missing out on prescribed chores may be required to do them at specific times in order to be supervised. The child or teenager who is out later than agreed with parents may have to stay at home next weekend.

A child can lose a favourite activity, a playtime or a privilege to help her towards more desirable behaviour, But NEVER humiliate her or cause her to be bitter. A complete accident by a careful child should not be punished. Don't make the punishment last longer than the memory of the initial action. Don't make a child pay for a whole window repair if this leaves him or her without money for months. If a teenager is being kept at home for coming in late, don't keep her in on numerous occasions. If she stayed out so long that parents see this as a major problem, start looking for the cause and together make a new plan in the order of her life in the family. Severe punishments can produce severe reactions; a child who is punished too severely will cease to believe in her own ability to be good, to please, or to do better. All corrective action should still fit with the positive message 'I believe in you and I know you can do better.'

Joint Decisions
As soon as it is feasible, develop a joint parent/child decision-making process. Find ways to decide together on the steps to be taken and the part each child can play. When things are talked over together the decisions become those that everyone can live with and will not be imposed by just some members of the family. Encourage active listening so every family member can tell her thoughts and feelings in a situation. Concentrate on statements that begin with 'I think' or 'I feel' rather than on judgements of another person. If adults offer judgement rather than statements about themselves, other members of the family will find it very hard to get beyond simply reacting defensively.

Disapproval
Children who have been institutionalised, who have perhaps been fostered or adopted, may not respond positively to disapproval. At heart they often see themselves to be unlovable, so when they feel your withdrawal, your disapproval, they interpret this as proof that you don't love them. Rather than being motivated to different behaviour to regain your affection, they withdraw further into themselves and may not change their actions. Such children require a different, though consistent, approach until they reach an awareness of parents' love. For this reason many of the organisations involved in adoption and fostering now provide programmes for new parents to help with such situations.

CORRECTION IN PUBLIC

All parents remember occasions when, in the middle of a busy shop, their child decided to scream furiously about something he wanted; or sitting in the house of a grandparent or elderly relative, they have heard loud and clear a fight going on

Correction or Punishment

between the children, producing an ominous 'Tut, tut' from the relative. Parents suddenly feel quite useless and that, with the whole world watching, there's nothing at all they can do except rush home. The truth is that most of the people in the shop, suddenly distracted from their business by the child's tantrum, have all been through the same thing. Rather than criticising, they are probably empathising and hoping that the parent will cope more gracefully than they did. Most people like most other people to succeed in what they are doing.

At home establish a routine for coping with a child's misbehaviour. Think out in advance how to cope in the same way when in a shop or crowded place. If you take your child out of the room at home, you may ask a shop supervisor to watch your trolley for a moment. Pick up your handbag or valuables and carry your child out of the shop into the open air. If you appear unflustered, so will the other customers be. Be firm and quiet. If they are simply demanding what you have decided they cannot have, and you have stuck to your word at home, it will be a quicker process in the shops.

Respect yourself as a parent and do not be put off by other people's expectations. Older generations may have raised children differently, but if you have thought through carefully what you are doing with your child, you need not be defensive. Before you go to grandmother's house prepare a bag of your child's favourite toys, perhaps include a new and intriguing one. Before arrival let your child know that there are more things than usual that she cannot touch or bump into. Let her know that you will correct him or her just as you do at home if she misbehaves, though you understand it is difficult in a new place. Older children can be told that you would specially like them to be on best form as granny is rather sensitive.

If grandparents tend to interfere, by being overtolerant or wanting parents to be much more strict, it can clear the air well if parents are open in their response. 'I know you are concerned for the children; I appreciate that. Dave and I have worked out how we will discipline them and would prefer to do it our way. I'm sorry if you disagree and are hurt by that.'

SUMMARY OF CORRECTION

The stages in constructive correction may be summarised:
- give a clear instruction
- tell the consequences of ignoring the instruction
- follow through on the consequences, doing so immediately

– stay present with love and affection, reassuring the child of your love.
– do not respond in anger and frustration, wait till you are calm and can think clearly.

PROBLEMS BETWEEN CHILDREN IN THE FAMILY

Families with more than one child are almost bound to run into the problem of sibling rivalry between the children.

Jealousy is common among children. A new baby arrives on the scene and a happy toddler suddenly becomes fractious and spiteful. A child who often demands attention and gets it can result in accusations from the other children that 'Mum loves him more than me.'

On a piece of paper list the last seven days. Under each write in the names of your children. Next to each name write in the time during which you gave them your undivided attention.

Saturday	Jane
	Martin
	Shelley
Sunday	Jane
	Martin
	Shelley
Monday	Jane
	Martin
	Shelley . . .

How much time did each of your children get? The youngest may still be more dependent on you for physical help, nappy changing and feeding, but the others still need a little of your time every day. It can be quite helpful, even if ages are fairly close, to separate bedtimes so each can have a brief time with you to talk about the day or hear you tell a story or just have

Correction or Punishment

a cuddle. It's the kind of time when the others should not be allowed to intrude.

When children come in from school they are often quite stressed, a few minutes with you talking and relaxing, sharing their day's frustrations can be very therapeutic. In a busy family try to make some space between children arriving home from school and the time they rush off to a music lesson or to Cubs. Whatever time it is, let there be a break when the child can talk easily, and relax from the pressure of the day.

When I was a child, in a family with four children whose ages were very close, we used to fight and tease one another. There was jealousy but looking back there were lots of other causes as well, some real and some imagined. I see the same kinds of pressures among other families today.

The youngest appears to the older children to get the best of many things, more tolerance over bedtimes, more money than they did, more time. The only boy, or only girl, among several children may appear a favourite and be resented by the others who will undoubtedly take it out on her.

When the ages of children are close together, they are at the same time struggling to negotiate socially with others. The tensions are greatest where the most negotiation is needed, where children share a bedroom, cupboards, bathtimes, chairs in front of the television, and all the other facilities of the home. Their inability will frequently end in fighting, more than with children from outside the family with whom they won't fight so often for fear of losing friends. But brothers and sisters won't be frightened off. The problem can be calmed somewhat by consistently separating children when they fight and using restrictions such as loss of privileges. In addition consistently request that children bring their dispute to an adult when they find that fighting seems the only next step, so the adult can help them talk till a solution is reached. Do not let boys get away with fighting any more than girls, the epithet 'boys will be boys' is only true in this instance because parents let it be.

QUESTIONS FOR INDIVIDUALS AND GROUPS

1. Note your own responses and questions to the section on punishing too severely p160, and on fighting among the children in a family p166.
2. What forms of correction or punishment were most effective in your childhood? Which did you most respect?

3. By what method do you correct your child, how effective is this?

QUESTIONS FOR GROUPS

1. Listen to one another's personal experiences of correction during their childhood.
2. When we consider correction it is helpful to look at how Jesus corrected others.

  Thomas: John 20:24–28
  Peter: John 18:25–27
  Zacchaeus: Luke 19:1–10
  A woman: John 8:3–11
  Pharisees: Luke 11:37–52

How would Jesus' correction have been viewed in his day? Was he following the norms of his time? Consider together what principles can be drawn from these stories today.
3. What methods are being used by members of the group with their children? What is their effectiveness as a means of changing behaviour? Discuss this as a group. Are some forms too harsh or too lax to be acceptable?
4. What forms of correction are acceptable for church settings, such as Sunday School? Should corporal punishment be used there or in schools?

Footnotes
[1] The NSPCC or local Social Services Department
[2] This section owes much to *The Needs of Children*, Mia Kellmer Pringle, Hutchinson, 1975
[3] *The Needs of Children*, Mia Kellmer Pringle
[4] *Ibid.*

16. VALUES AND LIMITATIONS IN SOCIETY

With so much consideration of values, of why and how parents can discipline and correct children, it seems everything should be straightforward. But it isn't. The mother who fought several court cases in her attempt to prevent doctors prescribing the birth control pill to girls under sixteen without parental consent, had a set of family values that were not supported by society around. This in turn meant that this particular parent could not be sure that she was being supported on a very fundamental issue of ethics and morality.

Many values in family life are supported by society; everyone expects children to go to school these days, and though there were differences of opinion when the school leaving age was raised to sixteen, now it goes without question. Society is structured toward keeping children at school, both in the family and in the local community.

Many factors in local community life are legislated to support family life, but there are aspects in which only the parents can be involved. In the normal course of events, community support involves general and well-established standards, such as the certificates that are allocated to films at the cinema so young children may not see unsuitable adult films.

However, there are no laws for video films or television. With regard to the latter, agreed codes within TV companies control the levels of violence and the quality of material. Not so with videos. Each parent has responsibility for seeing that the films their child sees are within reason and compatible with the values the parent espouses.

ADVERTISING AND TELEVISION

Using the following set of questions, sit with your child while she watches children's television one afternoon after school.

She may help you fill in the spaces. Watch for advertisements particularly. Underline the words below that represent the situations you see, and cross out the ones you haven't seen. Add other words of your own.

Homes. Spacious, very tidy, fitted kitchen, own garden, own car, expensive, untidy, overcrowded, flats, poorly furnished, dilapidated, poor . . .

Mother. Slim, elegant, well dressed, white, waiting for children, smiling, efficient, grumpy, fat, scruffy . . .

Children. Well-dressed, handicapped, scruffy, polite, well spoken, well behaved, lonely, unhappy, lots of children in the family . . .

The adverts will usually use the types of people that most watchers would want to be. Some programmes, especially dramas, may try to be more realistic.

Which of the following messages do you get from the toy adverts?
'You'd be happy if you had this toy'
'If your parents really cared they'd buy this for you'
'This is what you really need'
'This is what every child is getting this year'
'You'll never succeed without this'
'You must have the latest . . .'
What other messages are you given? Write some in.

Reconsider the pictures of homes. Consider the parents you saw. Of the words you have underlined or written describing

Values and Limitations in Society

the mothers you saw, circle the words that could describe you as mother, that describe your home, your spouse.

On the whole, advertising presents the images about which people fantasise, not what they really are. A lot of people would like to be the family in the ads, or the manufacturers would not use those pictures. But these are not *real* families in *real* homes. They are abnormal, imaginary, the person you would like to be if you could. They are also designed to make the viewer want what he or she doesn't have, whether a toy or a way of life. Just as much of the cigarette and alcohol advertising is built around sexual fantasies and macho images, so advertising for children is based on images, fantasies and caricatures. The result is that a child can become very disatisfied with what she does not have, with what her parents can't or won't give them. She will even become dissatisfied with the way her parents look or organise family life. When she says 'But everyone else's mum . . .', this may not be a reflection on the other ordinary mums who wait outside the school each day, but on the image presented on the screen. The people advertising don't mind creating this dissatisfaction in a child, as they are banking on the child persuading her parents to go out and buy the product.

If you are concerned about your discoveries, watch television with your child sometimes. Talk about the values of the ads and compare the people with real people the child knows, so her perspective can be broadened.

Whatever values you hold as a family, they are probably not well supported by advertising. In a wealthy society where many people have everything they *need*, sales depend on finding new products that the manufacturer can persuade people to *think* they need. Most are luxuries.

Consider too the advertising you watch and how it affects you. Look at the advertising in general magazines, or women's magazines, and assess how much they pressurise you to attain a perfect image. The advertised product is reputedly going to make you into what you want to be, but haven't yet managed.

List the advertising words used to sell toys for under-fives, and you end up with a projected image of what the good parent should be concerned about, for example, strong, safe, educational, washable. The words change for older children but the technique doesn't. If the ad is aimed directly at children it carries one particular image; if to the parents' it will appeal to their wanting the best for their children. The longstanding method of the door-to-door salesman with the children's encyclopaedia succeeds because parents can be manipulated on the basis of their concern for the children's future education.

Programmes

Television can be a significant intrusion into family life. Make sure there are times when the television is off and the children can freely occupy parents' time without being told 'Be quiet. Stop talking.' Only relaxed, easy-going times together result in children confiding in parents naturally.

In many families children watch several hours of television each day. Smaller children tend to watch the most. The problem is that these children then miss out on play and conversation.

Children learn when they talk and participate in activity. Television alone can teach children almost nothing. Educational programmes are successful when children have an opportunity to reflect and discuss what they saw, then undertake related activity. The television must never take the place of shared family time, of friendship and fun together. Consider the possibility of having the television on only when the whole family is going to watch a particular favourite programme together.

Several families I have known have experimented with leaving the television off for a week, to discover the effect. They have found that the members of the family see more of each other, talk together a lot more and tell one another about their daily experiences. But the pressure for having television is great, probably every family has a set, but don't forget that those who work for television are paid to persuade viewers to watch their programmes; they are not paid to look after family life; only parents can do the latter. Plan complete evenings without television for your family and consider having a celebration such as Christmas without any television.

The contents of the programmes themselves deserve some scrutiny. Many of the children's programmes have among the writers people skilled in considering the social and emotional effects of the material. The destructive and negative effects of drugs and drug-dealing was intentionally included in the programme, *Grange Hill*, to point out the truth to viewers who might be offered drugs in their own schools. Episodes include other aspects of life for young teenagers, as well as making some room for their aspirations and dreams. Parents may find it helpful to watch with their children occasionally, asking

Values and Limitations in Society

whether the situation is realistic, and find out more about how their children experience life outside the home.

Look out for the negative aspects of TV. Many family entertainment programmes put forward strange and unacceptable values for Christian parents. In the fight between good and evil which is a very common theme, children can accept that which is straightforward, reflecting their own ways of seeing justice in terms of polarities, of black and white. In family television programmes, check that the values are ones that parents would uphold. At times the level of violence and use of violence to achieve the aims of the hero or the villain, is unacceptable. Those who watch a lot of television develop some immunity to the presentation of violence so vigilance is necessary.

Similarly, increased public interest in the occult has resulted in this being shown more in television programmes; check that the programme presents this in a way that is compatible with Christian values. Approaches to moral values should be considered, and where for example relationships are represented check that qualities such as loyalty and integrity are affirmed. Some regular serialised programmes show fairly accurate representations of the pressures and tensions of everyday life. Within these some characters may be living out values that Christian parents could not endorse, but watching the programme with their children may be of greater value to the children than stopping their viewing.

FOOD FOR HEALTH AND GROWTH

There are two very strong forces working on our attitudes to healthy eating. One is the concern of medical and health experts, the other is the makers and sellers of food products.

Contemporary affluence had led society into over-eating and obesity has been a problem among young children to an unprecedented level. The concern of health experts expressed in magazines and books galore have caused parents to look for healthier ways of eating.

Food producers employ advertisers to maximise the sales of their product. Often they use health words to persuade us to choose their product: 'full of natural goodness'. But the consumer interest in healthier foods is reaching some supermarkets who are beginning to stock, for example, tinned fruits preserved in natural juice without sugar. Packages and cans also carry a full list of the contents.

Having heard the advice of the experts, parents can select

food that is going to be healthy for their children. As children grow, parents can create eating patterns that will help a child for the rest of her life. It may be worth that extra effort.

Deciding on a newer healthier pattern of eating requires a concerted effort. Favourite dishes are easy to cook because you have done them so many times. Even menus are based on longstanding habits. Looking at foods that children need for health the following is necessary.

Everyone needs:

Protein for body-building, growth, and repairing body cells.

Carbohydrates and **fats** for energy.

Fibre to keep a healthy digestive system

Iron for blood maintenance and vitality

Calcium for building and repairing teeth and bones

Vitamins for health and protection:

    A – for skin and eyes

    B complex – general health and nervous system

    C – for general health. (Works with iron)

    D – works with calcium

These vitamins and minerals can be found in the following foods:

Protein in cheese, eggs, beans and peas, seeds and nuts, cereals, meat and fish.

Carbohydrates and **fats** in dried fruit, nuts, butter, milk, sugar, honey, chocolate, margarine, oils, cocoa.

Fibre in wholewheat products, jacket potatoes, peas and beans, corn, mushrooms, fruit, especially berries.

Iron in eggs, baked beans, wholemeal bread, raisins, cabbage and other green vegetables, potatoes, cocoa, lentils, prunes, black treacle, and meats, especially offal.

Vitamins

    A in carrots, green vegetables, fats, apricots

    B in yeast, Marmite, peanuts and peanut butter, mushrooms, peas, oats, wheat, milk

    C in green vegetables, citrus fruits, tomatoes, blackcurrant and rosehip syrup

    D in eggs, cheese, butter, margarine, milk.

A balanced and appetising meal is fairly easy to achieve from all the above foods, and a balanced diet can be simply considered from the following chart.[1]

Values and Limitations in Society

Food groups
One: Milk, cheese, icecream, yoghurt
Two: meats, fish, eggs, peas and beans, nuts, peanut butter
Three: vegetables and fruits
Four: cereals and bread

During the course of a day a child should have at least one serving from each group. They should have up to four servings from group three and from group four. A young teenager will need more of group one than other age groups.

On an average day, considering the child has a packed lunch to take to school the following is possible:
Breakfast: cereal and toast with a glass of milk
Breaktime: apple or other fruit, or nuts and raisins, or 'muesli' style biscuit
Lunch: cheese, egg, meat spread or peanut butter sandwich, fruit if not at breaktime, chocolate biscuit
After school snack: fruit or raw carrot, nuts and raisins, muesli biscuit or Marmite sandwich
Supper/dinner: Potatoes in their jackets, green vegetables, meat or eggs or cheese dish, or casserole with beans or lentils. Ice cream with chocolate sauce.

Wholewheat sliced bread is a lot more filling than white bread and children who are used to it, prefer it.

Sugar is better used in moderation and at times near to teeth cleaning, not for snacks. When children first try tea and coffee make it very milky but give them no sugar. The same is true with cereals; most are fine without sugar if that's how a person is used to them. Don't put sugar in milk drinks like chocolate either. Select brands of drinking chocolate that have no added sugar.

Avoid fried foods, or keep them for special occasions. Don't have chips more than once a week; have jacket potatoes more often.

Give a child who is very hungry after school a nourishing sandwich with a protein filling like peanut butter, rather than a sweet one. Avoid chocolate bars for snacks as chocolate gives short bursts of energy followed by a low and a desire for more chocolate!

Additives
Many of the foods in our kitchen cupboard, especially tinned and preserved foods, contain more than expected. My bottle of blackcurrant and lemon contains: water, sugar, lemon juice,

blackcurrant juice, malic acid, vitamin C, natural flavouring, stabiliser (E466), preservatives (E211; E223), colours (E150, E123, E132), artificial sweetener, saccharin. The biggest ingredients are water and sugar, and once the list gets beyond natural flavouring, I begin to wonder what the other ingredients are. Many other labels show similar additives.

A number of adults in playgroups and health organisations have realised that additives such as those listed here affect children in adverse ways. A particular ingredient used to produce orange colour in squash, fish fingers, ice lollies, and other foods and sweet products, causes hyperactivity in many children. In the absence of statutory limits on their use, parents can select those products that are additive free.[2]

Convenience foods are not necessarily bad foods. No one wants to spend unnecessary time in food preparation. Tinned baked beans on toast are an excellent and nutritious meal; see what other foods that are quick and easy to prepare are within the limits of your healthy diet and then use them.

Snack foods are good if you select carefully. Most of us would be healthier on more smaller frequent meals in a day anyway. But do choose the kinds of healthy foods that are listed above. Don't make potato crisps in their many varieties, (or any other fried food) a major part of your child's eating pattern; keep them for an occasional party or treat.

When you have decided how and what to eat it's up to you to keep in mind the reasons for choosing this pattern. Look again at food advertising and see what you are being persuaded into buying. And don't too readily succumb to your child's conviction that 'everyone else has it'.

It's up to you to bring together your values and your limitations as a foundation for your child's health.

QUESTIONS FOR INDIVIDUALS AND GROUPS

1. Having studied the above questions on advertising if you did it alone, redo it with your child. Ask the extra questions below, to find out what your child thinks. Do not criticise her for her answers but recognise how effectively the TV advertising agencies did their work.

Which was the best mother we saw on the ads? If we had lots of money what should we buy? Of all the things advertised, which will make us happiest? What should I look out for next time I go shopping? If we were very poor, what would happen to us? Are the children like your friends at school? Which toys should every child have? Which toys were for boys? Which toys were for girls?

2. Over the next few days, watch several early evening family entertainment or adventure programmes.

Assess:

the moral message of the programme

the level of violence and for what means is it used

the life values that are affirmed by key characters, heroic and villainous

3. Do the results of your checking suggest any change in TV watching patterns?

QUESTIONS FOR GROUPS

1. As a group go over the results of the research of several days' TV by individuals.

What harmful and helpful aspects have been noted?

Are there changes that the group would wish to make to future viewing? How can these changes be achieved?

2. Are there particular programmes produced for family viewing that the group found to have disturbing contents?

In order that programme makers and distributors know what parents think about the contents of their programmes it would be helpful if the group together could send a letter to the producers or the TV channel concerned, expressing their views.

3. The determination of healthy attitudes and values take into account and reflect our culture and upbringing. Concerns about television and other media could obviously not affect the people of God in biblical times. However there are underlying principles that are present in biblical considerations of values that may well help our considerations today. Read the first two chapters of Proverbs, (individually you may wish to read further as much of this book is about values), and discover together any principles relevant to your own discussions. Consider not only which are relevant but *how* they are relevant and applicable in your daily lives.

Footnotes
[1] *More-with-Less Cookbook*, Doris Janzen Longacre, Lion.
[2] Look for books on additives among those on health and cooking at your local bookshop.

17. FAMILY WORK AND LEISURE

Family leisure
There are times, such as Christmas or on holidays, when a family has a common activity or interest that brings them together. What do these special family occasions give to us and our children?

Family celebrations help members feel good about belonging to one another, about being a family. Everyone, however much they enjoy having time alone, needs a family to which to belong. Adults, if they are not married and don't live close to relatives, may make their own 'family', finding just a few intimate friends with whom they can share everything. They have a wider circle of friends with whom they have common interests. Then there will be an even wider circle of acquaintants, people met at work and on social occasions or in the local community. Everyone needs those circles to be a fulfilled human being. For children the intimate friendships, that inner circle, is the life of the family. Adults may choose their close friends, those with whom they share dreams, hopes, fears, joys and sorrows. For children, the family, and particularly parents, is where they are dependent and where they find their first close relationships.

Family Time
Good reciprocal friendships are those in which we can give and take. Listen as well as talk. To really listen means you value what the other person has to say. You are interested in her, in her thoughts and feelings; your appreciate them. A small child wants to talk and be heard; she is not yet interested in listening. In being listened to, she receives the underlying message that she is alright, that what she thinks and says has value and she has the right to say it and be heard. The give-and-take comes next when the child also becomes a listener.

I had a friend whose small son, almost five years old, had

extreme difficulty sitting still and quiet to listen for even a minute. She asked me what I would do under the circumstances. Through our conversation I soon realised that Graham was never *expected* to listen. He spoke whenever he wanted to and she carefully listened. Even at mealtimes he managed to control conversation and would eventually get down from the table when he was bored. Her tolerance and love allowed him to continue to be self-centred long after he could have become more sensitive to others. It was time he learned to listen to his brother and parents when they had something to talk about. Together we talked about helping Graham listen. When the family said grace, Graham was required to sit still without grumbling or complaining, quietly waiting for his food with everyone else. It took some persistence but eventually the change became visible. He began to be interested in conversation with others. He began to ask questions.

Family mealtimes are a good opportunity for all members of the family to talk and listen, to the encouragement of all the members. Parents can ask questions that draw out quiet members, can encourage noisier members to be still at times. Children are helped by being present during conversation about circumstances that are beyond the scope of their everyday experience, about the factory, the shop or the office. What they don't understand they begin to question as their parents talk. But more importantly, they pick up the tenor of the conversation and the 'social graces' of talk-listen-talk-listen.

Listening with friendliness and concern, without competition with the television or one another, establishes a foundation for a child's growing years. She learns to share and expect interest from parents and family in the problems she meets, the sticky situations she gets into, and in the joys and successes of life. She learns to listen and to help others.

When a family chooses to relax together, to play together and to enjoy one another's company they are offering to one another some of the most important gifts of family life – those of belonging, of being wanted and loved.

When someone has a choice about how they spend their time and chooses to be with us we feel loved and affirmed. When a family chooses to do something that they enjoy doing together all of them are affirmed and encouraged. Think carefully of what all your family would enjoy. One father I know took his son into the woods at night to watch for deer. They stayed out all night, sitting in a tree. They saw no deer but had a great time being together. Another father and son go fishing together. When my daughter was in her teens we discovered how much we enjoyed the theatre together. Lots of families enjoy having an evening to play games together – *Scrabble, Monopoly* or *Trivial Pursuit*. Does your family ever tackle a jigsaw together?

Christmas and birthdays are good opportunities to give tangible expression of love to one another. Don't be trapped into thinking that money and the amount you spend is the measure of your love for one another. You may wish to buy presents but there are other values involved. Close friends and family often appreciate more than anything the home-made presents they receive. The key message is that you love them enough to spend your leisure time thinking of and making a present for them.

Match together your skills and the people concerned. Watch for your family's interests and needs and give a home-made present that pleases them and tells them you love them for who they are.

Teenagers experiment with being different from everyone else and family celebrations or leisure activities may be the last thing they would like to join. Continue to enjoy family life together, allowing the teenager the choice, to join in if she wishes to. She may find her own activity and places to go but often she will choose the family activity. Even after leaving home, as a young adult, she will still find enjoyment in being with the family as the opportunity arises.

Family Work

Children can experience two kinds of work in the family, 'family work' and 'paid work'. Different values as well as skills may be learned in these two broad categories.

Family work has tended in the past to have clearly-defined role-orientated categories. Children perceive these roles and act them out in the games of mothers and fathers that children play with their friends. Dads go out to work and earn the money, do the vegetable gardening, deal with cars and those household tasks that are considered the work of the handyman, such as mending fuses, decorating and unblocking pipes. Mums cook and clean, sew and shop, see to school affairs and generally order the children's lives.

The picture today may be considerably modified. Often both parents have full-time jobs outside the home. With present employment patterns women are often also needing to be wage-earners. Sometimes they are the only bread winners in the family and their new role obviously results in changes in attitude and patterns of family work.

Family work is that which a family does for itself, to maintain its own life, look after one another and the house and everything that is the family's together. Children benefit greatly by joining in the responsibility for family life, through helping with the work. The family belongs to all the members so the work that is involved in making this a happy family belongs to all the members. The question then is how to get the work done. But before looking at that, consider the benefit to the children of seeing that both the family's life and its work belongs to them.

Everyone has household work to do. Even if they choose to stay single there are still the ordinary chores to do. If adults choose to marry and have a family they have more responsibility and chores of a more varied kind, but maintaining daily living always involves work. Children can learn both what to do and how to do it by helping alongside their parents.

In the Christian Community to which I belong, a child's seventh birthday was, for a number of years, in addition to being a celebration, the time for their joining the washing-up rota. Not that a seven-year-old was very skilled at the work, but by working on a team she began to learn to tackle the task and be equally involved with a chore that is never a favourite but is a daily necessity.

It is at home that children can learn how to defrost the fridge, how to disinfect the toilet, how to clean the kitchen, how to keep plants and to dig the garden. When children are tiny it may be helpful for them to be out of the way when the kitchen is redecorated. But once a child reaches school age, there's lots she can help with while following through the steps of preparation with Mum and Dad. She can help get the paint charts from the shop, help consider colour matches and types of paint. A child sees the tools laid out and hears why they're all needed and what can be done with them. She can help clear out furniture that mustn't get spotted with paint. Some of the tasks she can help with, fetching, carrying, and washing down. Through helping a child learns the skills of cleaning, rubbing with sandpaper, and, when older, of painting. This is one only of the many aspects of family work that are models for the child of how to plan, prepare and undertake a work project at home.

A five-year-old can also creatively find out what she cannot do, where she is not skilled and discover what she will one day accomplish.

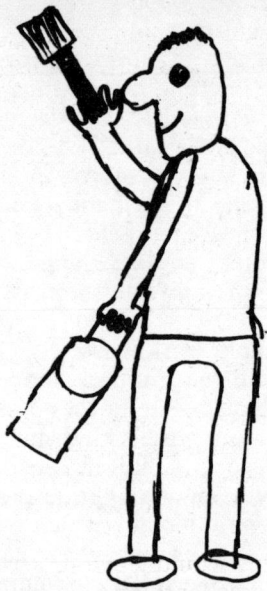

Explain how you see she is not yet able to tackle a particular task and tell her what she will learn and grow to in the next few years so he or she will then have the necessary skill.

There are many tools around the home that, because of their uses, are potentially dangerous – everything from sharp knives to electric drills. There are many accidents in homes because these are misused or placed irresponsibly. Children can gradually learn the skills of using them safely by working with their parents. Do not start children working with power tools whether for carpentry, hedge trimming or even sawing, before they are teenagers. They do not have the ability to foresee the dangers involved. But they may safely use hand tools before that.

Seeing a hard or heavy task completed affords great satisfaction to the person who has done it. I watched six-year-old Matthew work alongside his dad for several hours moving rubble to make a hard core to their drive-way. He was extremely pleased with his day's work and felt satisfied.

It's an asset for the parent to be able to cultivate the habit of thinking out loud while planning, preparing, and doing the work. The child alongside him hears what's involved and when she doesn't understand can ask a question. So the experience is a pattern of actions and words, a constructive learning model. When you meet a problem in the work, raise it as a question. While the child may have few answers for you, she does experience your creative problem solving.

Once the novelty has worn off, what then? Should the child continue with the work and if so why? Every child, because of age and aptitude, has more or less ability to complete a task. In the end parents have to assess the situation according to the child. But there are significant pointers to hold in mind. Carrying on after reaching boredom is part of responsibility. Life always involves irksome tasks and no one should grow up expecting to do only what she feels like doing or completing only those tasks that still entertain. Our children can learn that life requires some tasks that they'll hate from beginning to end. There are other tasks that we begin for our enjoyment and can set the finishing time ourselves, but we have to learn for the sake of everyone to clear up after ourselves, whether toys or tools. As the family divides up its work, a child may volunteer to do a particular task and in this case should see it finished. To give up in the middle would leave someone else with more work and a child should be learning to follow through faithfully on her own commitments. Sometimes a child wants to tackle a task at a particular time and is interrupted or the task is longer than anticipated. The child can come back to the family and discuss a new plan for completing the work. Parents let their child down if they do not depend on her to finish the work. If a child is having difficulty an adult may offer to help, but should avoid taking over or doing it for her.

The planning of family work and chores should take into account everyone's individual work schedules and skills.

Make a list of all the family members. Next to each name fill in the details in the table below. Ask your family to help you fill it in.

Name	Work outside home	Work brought home	Free time	Family work
Maggie	9–5		None	
Helen	School 9–4	Homework		

Fill in the chart as this fits your family, particularly the first three columns. Now make another list of family work to be done, as below.

Everyday	Weekly	Occasional	Projects
Cooking	Clean bathroom	Clean car	Build shed
Washup		Window-cleaning	Wash curtains
Tidy living room			

Look at your first list with your family. Fit the tasks of your second list onto the first, opposite the name of whoever volunteers to get the task done. *Talk about this together as you go*. People who choose their own tasks fulfil them better. Children need more playtime than adults, but adults who have no personal leisure time, or time alone, are unhealthy. Everyone should have some time off. In most households Mum gets trapped into being the one who does all the left-over tasks, filling all the gaps and covering for everyone else. Does this happen in your family?

Filling in a chart helps a family reassess how it does its work and how different members are responsible. You may only need to fill in a chart like this once, that may be enough to get the family sharing out responsibility and work. An informal conversation over the mealtable may be enough.

Paid work has a place in the family but chores that maintain family life should not be rewarded with money. Consider paying children for work that helps a family business, as they see the adults drawing money in return for their work.

Pocket money, whether or not it is earned by the child, is a helpful beginning in learning responsibility for money. With small amounts the child learns to make choices and to appreciate the relative values of different products. When a child is first given pocket money it is best to leave the child with complete choice of how that money is spent. It is tempting to give a child a pound and want her to save fifty pence of it in a bank account. If it is important to parents for the child to have some money in the bank, it is better that they tell her they are putting fifty pence in the bank for her and give the child only fifty pence for her own choice. To give her the money but telling her how to use it is only a pretence at giving real responsibility; she may learn to accept the *fait accompli* but will not have learned responsibility. A child best learns to save when she wants to buy something that costs more than one week's money and can only get that item by saving some money till the next week.

Encourage older children who want to get a paid job outside the home, such as a paper round or a Saturday job. Through such work children learn how to relate to employers, schedules and routines. Allow a child who earns money considerable choice over how it is used but do expect her to pay for her own entertainment and perhaps contribute to her own clothing needs. A teenager who earns several pounds may buy accessories or clothes for going to discos while parents continue to buy essential items including school uniform and shoes. Once a teenager begins a full-time job she should be paying a realistic contribution to the household budget as well as providing for her own clothes and entertainment.

The Local Community

The local community is much more help to a family than it is a hindrance. The health and life of the family is affirmed, supported and encouraged in the local community. In years gone by families lived more effectively in a form of extended family with relatives and friends, with all the attendant benefits, networks of friendship, protective familiarity and common experience. Since employment and social patterns have changed considerably a lot of that community experience has to be established by choice by parents, it is not there automatically. Making the effort to get involved in local life may be encouraged by realising what that local life can give positively.

To which of the following can you say yes? Put a tick in the appropriate column.

It is easy to fall into the trap of looking to involvement with your neighbours and local community only in those aspects in which you need specific help with your family. Medical care is an example. But it is in the local community that your family will find friendship and fun, as a family.

Each of the adults in your family may have friends in various places in the country; you may have moved house or been at college together. The children will play and find friends among those with whom they go to school and meet on the streets. All these are personal friends that will be special to each of you.

                                              yes   no

I know my next-door-neighbours
The people in my street are all friendly
I know the shopkeepers by name
I know who to go to for information about:
   district nurse
   primary schools
   parent teacher organisations
   playgroups
   residents' association
   local fete committee
   local carnival organisers
   sports facilities
   Brownies/Cubs
   councillors
   church leaders
   drama groups

Each family will know other families with whom the whole family is friendly. Family friendships are encouraging to both families. Values are affirmed, there is opportunity for conversation and play with others of similar interests. Often families will organise relaxation together, a barbecue in the garden, a walk, a swimming party. The effect on the family is to help everyone relax and enjoy themselves, just for the fun of it. When at a barbecue in someone else's garden you are not under pressure from your own work and chores, you can laugh and 'let your hair down'.

Everyone needs the opportunity to celebrate, away from work and everyday schedules. Often a local community has traditional celebrations that bring all the local people together. In the village where I grew up there were two fetes each year, to which all the village went. There were stalls and competitions that raised money for the village hall and parish church. We had sports for children and adults. We stayed for tea, heard who had won the Prize Draw and the evening was spent country dancing. Even the busiest people stopped their work, closed the village shop, and only absolutely essential work happened, such as milking the cows and collecting the eggs.

Such events brought together people of different backgrounds and walks of life, the rector, the farmer, farm workers, mechanics, housewives, and children. But the celebration belonged to everyone. Friendships were affirmed, neighbours

Family Work and Leisure

and acquaintances chatted and inquired about each others' children, health and changing circumstances.

Traditional communities, villages and towns all over the world have such celebrations in fetes, carnivals, and festivals. Their common participation in the life of the area, their friendships and interconnectedness comes together and is affirmed. Probably the most significant asset of such events is that all ages, all generations and all walks of life come together to enjoy themselves. The family is not compartmentalised into age-groups with a generation gap but, in that all join the celebration together, the family itself is affirmed.

When individuals choose friends, they choose through common interests or personalities. At a community event all kinds come together. People who don't like each other, have opposite interests, the lonely and the old, all belong to the gathering. The loss of such events to family life and members of a local community is to increase loneliness and isolation. Contemporary events are set up by organisations who want to raise funds for their common interests and have some value to a local community.

Are there local festivals where you live? Take special interest in events in your local community over the next few months and see how much you can include your family in the celebrations. Join in fancy dress competitions, building a float, or setting up a stall. Become part of the fun of the local community in which you live. You will find that the community will support you with your children as they get to know you, and you will find good neighbours who chat and encourage one another.

Street Parties

In urban areas where a local community is less easily defined, participation may not bring familiarity; there seem to be many strangers at the carnivals and festivals.

Consider starting a celebration that can bring neighbours together. In some areas of the country people from one street come together for parties, to celebrate Guy Fawkes or hold a fete. Could you invite your neighbours to a party? It is unimportant that you don't know them, you soon would. It does not matter that they are not your 'kind of people', a community celebration is special because a variety of people come together. Focus your event around a barbecue to which everyone can bring sausages for cooking on the grill and rolls to eat them with, and drinks that can be added to a drinks table for everyone. Alternatively, everyone can bring a 'pot' of their favourite supper that is put on the supper table and everyone can choose from all that's brought. Play games together or lead folk dances that even small children can enjoy.

The church
Many local churches function as a kind of local community. Becoming a Christian is about joining the community of God's people. So being in the church is not about attending church for personal satisfaction or only for Sunday worship but becoming part of a 'family' that cares for all aspects of the life of the members.

In my own local church we have had picnics with games in a local park, coffee mornings, annual Christmas pantomimes, and occasional evenings of folk music put on by the members. People of all ages have been included and have benefited from the ongoing belonging to this community. There is neighbourliness that includes friendship with older members, and as they have grown too old and infirm to get to church, friends from the church have visited them.

Interest groups
Some sports and social centres are organised so that whole families can become involved. Swim or walk together with other people, without separating the members of your family. Enjoy life together.

Most of all look for opportunities for your whole family to have fun together in a larger local community; you can together enjoy meeting and getting to know many different people who are linked to you by their belonging to the same local life.

QUESTIONS FOR INDIVIDUALS AND GROUPS

1. Make a note of family celebrations that you remember from your childhood. What did you enjoy most?
2. What are the special festive occasions you enjoy with your children now?
3. Are there local occasions to which you go as a family? What local community involvement do you have?

Are there church social gatherings to which you can go together?

Family Work and Leisure

QUESTIONS FOR GROUPS

1. Collect from the group their reflections on family celebrations.
2. Celebration and festivity were important elements in biblical society. Read John 2:1–11, Nehemiah 12:27–43, and II Samuel 6:12–19. These are all celebrations of common or uncommon events. Are there parallels in our Christian life today? What rituals and celebrations support our life, and the life of local communities, that celebrate our religious occasions and our more ordinary human existence? For example at a wedding we have a church ceremony and a party, for us the latter is as important as the former: Jesus provided the means for the party to continue. What structures and traditions supported these events in biblical times; what supports and facilitates them today?
3. Together list the local events with which members of the group are connected, such as Carnival committees.

Do these provide you with sufficient contact in your neighbourhood?

Are additional opportunities needed? If so what would you recommend?

4. Can your group, stimulated by this concern, organise a party or social gathering? Alternatively could your church organise such events?

18. CHILDREN'S FEARS

A baby enters a world of new, exciting and strange experiences. Some are very comforting, like the arrival of Mum when she cries. Having come from the darkness of the womb, a baby is suddenly in a bright and glaring world to which she has to adjust before she can learn to focus her eyes or make sense of her surroundings. A baby was protected, too, from loud sounds, and a sudden noise can reduce the baby to tears. As she grows she may well show fear at sounds and occurrences she does not understand.

For the first few months of life, a child has no idea that things exist beyond her own sight and hearing; she does not have the facility to imagine that her parents may be doing something she can't see. Mum simply reappears at times that seem related to her cries. So it is possible for the baby going into hospital to believe that since her cries do not bring Mum she is lost. Many babies in hospital go through a very painful emotional transition when they are reunited with their parents to begin to trust them not to disappear again. For this reason many hospitals now have facilities for a parent to stay with the baby in hospital.

But fears are about more than what is lost. At first a small child does not realise that cars won't come onto the pavement and indoors. They do not know that clouds stay in the sky, these swirling white creatures may come right down into the garden. She doesn't know that there are no strange creatures hiding in the dark cupboard just as she believes there is a lion in the garden; a small child is really afraid of sliding down the plughole with the bath water.

Only experience will show a child the order by which every creature and thing lives. Like a train on its tracks, everything has its way to be and its place to go. They will discover eventually that their body has a fixed shape, which means the plughole is far too small to be of danger. Lions live in the zoo and not in the garden; they realise after seeing the animals in the appropriate places, and finding that they stay there.

With so much unknown territory, a child is often over-

Children's Fears

whelmed by feelings of fear and danger. It can help for her to see the real source of noises; but like peoples throughout history a child may attribute a fearsome form, such as a dragon, to the strange noise. Many children wake up having had bad dreams, still terrified, scarcely aware of the difference between the images of the dream world and the reality to which they wake up. When people have their hair cut or put on clown make-up a child is afraid, until she is several years old.

Children simply grow out of some fears and hardly notice where they went; like the fear of the clouds or of the plughole. Other fears are melted away as someone explains that the pavement is for people and the road for cars, and people keep to the pavement to be safe. Other fears carry on much longer, sometimes because there is a real foundation to them, or an experience that causes the child to realise it was worth being afraid.

All children have fears and continue to discover new ones throughout their growing years. Each will ebb and flow, even the old common fear of spiders and creepy insects. Fears, while disturbing, are a normal part in a child's growth.

DEALING WITH FEARS

Parents are strong and powerful people. Daddy, coming into the bedroom of a fearful child, can order a fierce creature to go away and never come back. He can reassure the child that since he is sitting downstairs he will make sure no fierce beasts come in through the front door.

Irrational fears are not necessarily helped by adult attempts to rationalise them away. A frightened child in the heat of the moment will not readily believe that there are no weird creatures. She will eventually check on all sorts of things she fears and may want to work the hoover for herself to prove that she can overcome her fears.

A parent can be a helpful friend in the midst of fear. Because you are trusted, a child will tell you her secret fears, and regardless of how irrational these fears seem to you, they are very serious to the child so don't laugh. Treat a small child gently as you help her overcome them. Comfort the child and take her to a different place, to another room or into the light, till she is calm.

Sometimes a child is ready to face the source of the fear; more often she will have to prepare herself for such a step. Let her choose the time, and do not pressurise her or you may make the fear worse. You can then offer to face her fear with her, opening the cupboard together and making sure there is nothing inside.

In a family a child sees other members face their fears. It can help if they know that others are afraid sometimes and see how *they* face their fears constructively.

Most adults still have fears, maybe as nightmares or phobias. Think about yourself. What is it you are really irrationally afraid of? Is it spiders, or mice or worms? Are you afraid of dogs or cats? Are you afraid of the dark? If you tend to be afraid of thunder storms, find a way to cope with your fear — don't drag your child into the cupboard under the stairs with you! While one may need to be cautious of strange cats or dogs, parents should be communicating caution rather than handing on fears.

FEAR OF SEPARATION

It is fairly normal for a child at almost any stage to fear the loss of those she most loves. Even adults at times of anxiety can find themselves fearing the loss of a partner or relative.

In the tiny child such fear may be expressed by clinging to mum whenever she is slightly unsure of the situation. This may be triggered by an obvious circumstance, such as a time spent in hospital when a child really loses her security, or may be for no apparent reason. Even when able to talk well the child may not be able to offer a reason for her fear. The fear is none-the-less real and should be treated with respect. The clingy child is not necessarily helped by forced separation.

Whenever a child shows signs of such fear be very careful when leaving her with someone else!

Say clearly where you are going. Say clearly when you will return. Say clearly who is looking after her in your absence. She will probably cry when you leave so make sure that the person who cares for her knows where to get hold of you if the child does not get over her tears fairly quickly. It is unhelpful to leave a child too long if she is extremely distressed.

Avoid trying to leave when she is not looking. This simply affirms her fear, telling her it's best not to let you out of her sight or she may lose you again. She will also sense that she cannot trust you as you try to reassure her. Be very honest and tell your child even though she will cry while you are there rather than after you leave.

Check that the person with whom you leave the child is really

Children's Fears

sympathetic with a child's fear and will comfort and reassure her just as honestly as you have, hugging her and telling her you will be back to collect her later.

Playgroup leaders are experienced in helping children over this stage. Talk to them about your concerns.

Older children may show signs of such fear at other times of change. After marriage breakdown they may find it difficult to trust the word of the remaining parent and fear losing him or her also.

With all such fears be as honest as possible and as reassuring as possible. Above all take the stage seriously, thus laying a more secure foundation for the future.

19. DEATH

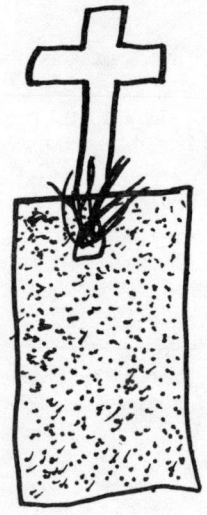

A death in the family affects all the members. If the death is of a relative or family friend, the event may seem to affect some more than others, for example, parents more than children. Yet if one family member is in the midst of grief, the others will be touched as well. With the death of a person close to all the family, someone with whom each member has her own relationship, the whole event will be a kind of family crisis, a shared event and a shared grief. Just as members express love and joy differently, so they will feel and express grief differently.

Being prepared
A child should know what death is before it happens to someone she loves and to whom she is close. To a small child death is an extremely hard concept to grasp, at least in its finality. She will expect it to be a temporary state. A child has little sense of passing time and will tend to suppose that 'dead' is much the same as gone-for-a-while. Illustrate your explanations

Death

with toys or equipment that are broken and won't work again. If a pet dies, help the child see that it is not going to live any more, and let her help to bury it.

When you are out for a walk include going through a churchyard or graveyard and point out the tomb stones and how long the people have been dead and buried. Explain what happened to them. An older child, over school age may want to know more about what happens to a body when someone dies, what is it that stops, or what is it that keeps some of us going. The teenager will be asking more philosophical and religious questions about the meaning of life.

Parents should tell the truth. Try to state clearly the difference between death, sickness and sleep. Sickness is a time when the body is struggling to get itself better, mend itself with medicines or operations, or simply fighting a cold. Sleep is the body taking a rest so it can wake up refreshed. People recover and come back from both these states. Don't confuse your child with explanations in which death sounds like sickness or sleep. Don't simply say, 'Grandpa was very sick and died in the hospital; he won't ever come back,' or when Mum goes into hospital to have a baby, the child will be dreading her death, for hospital and death go together. Do not say that death is going to sleep for a long time or the child may be afraid of sleep.

Death can be talked about gently and caringly – but truthfully. Yet society has euphemisms for death that attempt to hide the harsh reality.

Add phrases you have heard to the list below:
'She's gone away for a long long time . . .'
'He's pushing up the daisies.'
'His number was up.'
'She's passed away.'

Write down any phrases you have already used to describe death to your child. In what situations have you spoken to her about death? Would it be helpful to add additional explanations for your child?

Consider the members of your family. Each person would respond differently to a death. How would you tell each of them truthfully about death. Decide how you would start off telling them, and then you could let the conversation take its own course.

Every living thing will die one day. Just as it's essential to be able to talk about birth and other normal experiences, we must talk about and accept death together openly.

The event of death

When a death happens it is going to be painful for you and for the family; take time to tell each adult and each child on her own. This way each will be able to respond emotionally or with questions as she wishes. Many of the first thoughts or feelings may seem strangely detached, but each will have her own way of reacting and coping.

A small child will usually have very little to say, sensing the strong feeling in others and not realising the implications herself. She may not ask what happened to the person. Her questions may appear insensitive, but don't expect them to have an adult response. Be truthful without being unnecessarily detailed. If Grandpa was very old and his body was wearing out, explain this so that the child can see that this was why his heart stopped. Then the child will not worry about the hearts of other family members.

A school age child may want the actual details, even of a car crash, despite them being quite distressing. Answer any questions gently, receiving the mixture of questions and feelings she will have jumbled together.

A teenager will respond much as an adult and will be wondering why it was her father or grandfather who had to die now. She must process this question for herself; do not try to short-circuit her coming to a resolution by offering the resolution to which *you* have come. To offer 'God must have decided', expecting your child to be satisfied with this answer, may only result in the child feeling angry at God and guilty at her own grief. Such truth will gradually be resolved later in the family's and the individual's grief process.

As people come to terms with grief at the death of someone they love, all sorts of feelings may spill out from every member of the family. Some may be prone to making extra noise or laughing inappropriately.

Keep the routine of the day for a small child as near to normal as possible. A small child finds security in routine, as well as in people, and will suffer greater distress if all the stable patterns of life seem to change at once. She may seem to express few feelings in words or tears, even for the death of someone as close as a parent, but may well go through unusual actions. She may sit staring when she would usually be active. She may make a small movement repetitively, banging, sliding, or humming. A child will probably want more comfort and expression of affection than usual. It happens occasionally that a small child will, like one who's older, blame herself for the loss of a parent. With no way to tell a parent, she may become very withdrawn and quiet, very undemonstrative. You may wish to reassure her that the death wasn't her or anyone else's fault. While your words may have little effect (as blaming oneself is not a rational response) you may, through your tone, offer comfort and release for the child's feelings.

A school-age child will be more conscious of the effect of the loss of the dead person on her own life. Plans they had together will be considered and even anger expressed by the child at being let down. This may sound selfish, but, this is a child's way of recognising, then coping with, the changes in life now that the person is no longer there. Remember *active listening*, and encourage the child to say what she feels as she feels it. Tears are all part of the expression of loss, so do not try to stop a child crying.

Share your feelings as an adult. Your child can then understand and appreciate the sadness of others at the loss of this person. Death itself is not painful: it may be the end of pain for the person, but those who are left feel the pain of their absence, the pain of not having them in the family's life. Only gradually will the family get over these feelings as they establish a new life without the missing member. But first they live with the space where the loved one was with them.

Avoid allowing children to see the complete breakdown of one of their parents; this should not be shared. For a child, parents are stability and security, and they depend on parents maintaining a hold on order and reality. If the death is of husband or wife, invite someone else to help with the children for a day or two so the remaining parent can feel and express the depth of her own grief without causing undue stress for the child.

The funeral

As a family, go over what will happen now that someone has died. The child may have a variety of questions, depending on her age. Where is the body? What is happening to it? Talk about these together. A child may wish to go to see the body before the coffin is closed. While people today tend to avoid this experience for children, this reaction may be a result of society tending to pretend that death is avoidable. When a dead person used to be laid out in her own house and the coffin placed in the front room, grief was expressed more readily; it was less repressed. In hiding death, we have limited our ability to cope with it.

Look through the funeral service together. Consider what the service is for: it is a kind of goodbye from family and friends, a time to express together appreciation for the person and his life, and to mourn his loss.

Children may have questions about the property of the deceased person. What will happen to his house, his dog, his clothes and other belongings? Explain what a will is, so the child understands how this represents the person's particular bequests. Many children and young people would appreciate having a keepsake that reflects their own relationship with the one who died. Its financial value is unimportant, as they will treasure it for the memories it keeps alive.

When a family has lost someone close, expect overreactions of all kinds for quite a while afterwards. Some members of the family will be unusually active and at other times extremely depressed. Encourage each other, including the children, to be tolerant, or feelings may erupt into anger and frustration with one another.

If one of her parents died a child will go through many unconscious processes, like looking out of the window or repeating actions which they associate with the lost parent. Be tolerant. Talk about the dead person, of events you remember together. Recall parties and celebrations, funny events you all enjoyed. Remember his mannerisms and jokes. Remember his favourite places to visit, his favourite clothes. To remember these and be conscious of the cause of your grief will help the grief to be expressed without guilt, or feeling that 'we should have got over it by now'.

20. MARRIAGE BREAKDOWN

In her book *The Needs of Children*, Mia Kellmer Pringle[1], reflecting on the stability needed by growing children, goes so far as to suggest that those who wish to marry be encouraged to wait till they are twenty-two or more. Then they may be better able to cope with their own relationship as well as with children, thus reducing the possibility of parental breakup. She continues:

'Should there be two kinds of marriage? One would be a simple contract – designed to protect the interests of both partners in case of break-down – which could be readily terminated at the request of either. The other contract would involve a much more binding commitment . . . because the couple were wishing to raise a family and were prepared to put the needs of their children for stability and continuous, loving care above their own need for self-fulfilment; this contract would be much more difficult to terminate.'

In this way one of the most respected voices in the field of children's rights, care and growth recognises and challenges her readers with the seriousness with which a marriage with children should be viewed.

Marriages between couples who marry in their teens are statistically more likely to break down and end in divorce, as the struggle to cope with the issues of money, housing and stability overwhelms them. Many would-be parents have not considered the sacrifice of time, energy, money, career, and freedom of choice that is essential to raising children. And those who have thought that having a child would cement together a rocky relationship have found this to be untrue.

Children form a strong relationship with both parents; their sense of security, of stability and self-esteem are based on the relationships they have with both. Trust, and the knowledge of being loved unconditionally, are shattered when the children lose a parent, apparently at the parent's choice. Often in the midst of a crumbling marriage there is accusation and counter accusation, resentment and bitterness between parents, and often this is repeated to the children or used to influence or evoke the child's support. It is extremely destructive to the child and causes permanent marking on her own relationships, including her marriage when she reaches adulthood.

The loss of a parent in marriage breakdown is like a death. A young child, not realising the significance of the tensions and arguments, will register the same depth of confusion and loss as if the parent had died. The pressure of the arguments and criticism (or the sudden silence as she walks in on arguments) will cause many children to believe themselves to be the cause of the breakdown. The child may be desperate to find a solution so she can keep both parents, and may be angry with herself that she cannot. Her sense of self-worth and self-trust will deteriorate.

The grief process associated with separation and divorce is long. Not only does the loss of the person have to be reconciled, the dependent child has also lost something of herself that was attached to this parent, something that was broken and betrayed in the loss. While a death takes away a parent, a divorce is an active rejection, a choice to not have the child. A child's behaviour may be quite disturbed, expressed in outbursts of aggression or simply by a quiet withdrawal.

At different ages the response may be different. Some understanding helps the child feel less guilty and confused. Children under five seem to suffer most as there is virtually no rationalising process to help them cope. In this latter respect, a boy's concept of father, man and husband may be imprinted with the broken relationship he experiences when losing his father.

Children approaching adolescence are launching themselves into their own identity from the foundation of safety and security at home. To break that security and trust at the point at which they begin to struggle with their own identity effectively pulls the rug out from under them. Losing her father, an adolescent girl may doubt her own ability to form good relationships with men.

However, for many adults and children, the breakdown of a difficult marriage may be a relief, bringing to an end the bitterness and recriminations. Without the possibility of agreement between parents, children may have had to suffer differing standards of discipline. It is a relief when the limits are consistently set. At times the parents, in being dissatisfied with one another, are also dissatisfied with the children and may have been communicating this to them for a long time.

Once the pressures are declining and the first steps of the separation are completed, it is vital that the child has continued access to both parents so she can be reassured of continued love. The child's choice to spend time with both parents should be honoured as she reorganises and renegotiates her foundations for emotional stability and maturity.

Other changes during marriage breakdown should be kept to a minimum for the children's sake. There may be financial pressure, but try not to compound the situation with a child having to move home, change school and neighbourhood as well. Schooling will undoubtedly be affected, by the amotional stress the child experiences. Try to minimise this by explaining to the school so teachers are sympathetic toward the child's inability to concentrate. A sympathetic listener in a friendly teacher or school counsellor may be helpful to a child who wants to talk to someone who isn't taking sides.

LONE PARENTS

Ninety per cent of lone parents are women, only ten per cent are men. Some lone parents are widows and widowers while the majority are those whose marriage has ended with separation or divorce. The beginning of lone parenting is therefore nearly always marked by trauma or failure or both. Grief will accompany the crisis produced by a sudden change in circumstances. (Only a very tiny proportion of parents have consciously planned to bring up children alone, without initially parenting with a partner.)

A time of transition allows for the expression of grief, without which repressed feelings would continue to hamper the family in the future. All offers of help with practical matters are worth consideration, even though the parent is determined to stand on her own two feet in providing for her children. She should give herself a break in which to express her feelings to a sympathetic friend or professional counsellor and allow herself gradually to pick up the reins again. She should look for financial help from Supplementary Benefit, at least for a transitional period even if she does intend to be a full-time wage-earner.

Drastic change makes everyone in the family more vulnerable emotionally and in the long run there is a danger that the lone parent will be overly protective of her child and will lean on her too much emotionally. Particularly as children reach their teens parents should not be over-restrictive, making sure they have the freedom to develop their own life, even though the parent may be afraid of her own loneliness. She should look for her own friendships among peers as the children grow older.

Money

Of all lone parents, only fifty per cent of women and thirty per cent of men depend on State Benefit as their chief source of income. All the others depend primarily on their own earnings. Most are working full-time outside the home. This is an amazing feat when one considers they are also running a home and taking full charge of children's lives.

Women are at a disadvantage in the labour market. They receive lower wages than men and are more liable to take unskilled work. Also they are normally the ones who have taken and continue to take total responsibility for children. Lone fathers more often have the help of female relatives. Lone mothers are more likely to have pre-school children than lone fathers, so are more concerned to be at home with the children. All lone parents are likely to earn less than their two parent counterparts as they are less able to manage overtime or weekend work. But all parents on low income who work full or nearly full time should check on Family Income Supplement and similar benefits which can help quite considerably. This particular benefit is available only to those who are working.

Supplementary Benefit does not increase with time, so many lone parents find that, in effect, they are getting poorer. Low wages for part-time jobs discourages parents from taking them as there is an equivalent loss of Benefit. However, it is well worth investigating training or retraining so that as the children grow parents are able eventually to look for a semi-skilled or skilled job that pays better. Again, to take a job even though low-paid, and then apply for Family Income Supplement may bring the total above the Supplementary Benefit level.

New experience

All children need lots of opportunity for new discovery and new experience. The child of a lone parent, who is at home every day needs additional outside stimulation. Spending so much time together can inadvertently result in a higher level of emotional dependence or insularity for the child; it is necessary for the child to meet others and establish new relationships.

For a small child, new experiences of play and people can come through spending time with other adults, grandparents or family friends, even if the friends have no children of their own. Going to playgroup or nursery school is a great help to under-fives, there they have the opportunity to meet new adults and children, as well as having the opportunity to play with toys and equipment that could never be provided at home.

Childcare for the children of a parent who is working fulltime is probably harder to find. Some areas of the country do have nursery places available. Otherwise, look for registered childminders. These are people who have satisfied the local authority of their ability to look after other people's children in their own home. Very few employers provide any kind of childcare programme for employees' children but bigger companies may do so as they realise that such a programme would help their staff considerably.

Once children have started school it is hard to find somewhere for them to go till the parent gets home from work. The local Citizens Advice Bureau may know of after school programmes, though these are few and far between. Gingerbread, an organisation that is run for lone parents, has some facilities in various parts of the country.

If you are to be at work past the time that your child comes home from school and if the house is empty, make sure of several things.

– She knows how and whom to contact in an emergency. This is made easier if you have a phone in the house; place a list of phone numbers on the wall near the phone.

– There is a neighbour she could go to with a problem, such as a lost key.

– The type of heaters you use are safe for an unattended child.

– The child knows what she may or may not do in your absence, for example, cooking, going out, helping herself to food and so on.

– Your child will not answer the doorbell in your absence except by pre-arrangement with you. She may inadvertently let a stranger know she is alone in the house.

With growing numbers of lone parents recognising that there is a legal restriction on leaving children alone in the house, lone parents can club together to provide their own workable alternative. One or more parents in a group may, having no full-time job, have the other children come to her house after school. In return, the other parents would pay a contribution that covers time and costs, such as a snack when the children arrive. Gingerbread and other organisations for lone parents may have helpful suggestions on how to organise this. Look up one-parent organisations in your local library.

Housing

Many lone wives coping with marriage breakdown find to their horror that the house they live in is owned in the name of their husband, or is let to the husband by the council. They may have no right to continue to live there. Before taking *any* action contact the local Citizens Advice Bureau or Child Poverty Action Group, so that you do not mistakenly get categorised as voluntarily homeless – and therefore cannot qualify for help. In some areas a family who moves into winter-let holiday flats is considered voluntarily homeless; in other areas to turn down a particular council flat or house, because you don't like the neighbourhood, will also make your family 'voluntarily homeless'. To turn down the offer of accommodation with relatives may also have the same result. There is a tendency among local authorities to consider lone parent families, especially those headed by a woman, as problem families and to treat them accordingly. Take care and take advice.

Illness

Many lone parents, trying to cope alone and having just been through the breakdown of their marriage, are distressed and depressed. The stress they have financially, housing and other aspects of family life, means they live with greater stress than most other parents.

They worry a great deal over what to do about the possibility of illness. If the child is ill they may have to lose time at work and risk losing their job. If the parent is ill or even taken into hospital, what can happen to children when there are no willing relatives to help? Foster parents can be arranged at very short notice if a parent is rushed into hospital. They care for the child until the parent is fit again. One myth that should be dispelled is that children cared for this way may be taken from the parent permanently by local authorities who may consider the lone parent unfit to cope. There is very little danger of this happening due to illness, homelessness or poverty.

Prejudices and myths

Lone parents are a burden to the welfare system and therefore a problem – **false**. More than half of all female lone parents support their family themselves, despite the fact that women's wages on average are only seventy per cent of men's wages. Seventy percent of male lone parents continue with their job.

A child needs his mother at home, but a lone father should work – **false**. A child has the same emotional needs whether the remaining parent is male or female, and the sex of the parent is immaterial. The lone parent takes on all the responsibility of parenting, usually shared by a man and a woman, and struggles to balance those out as best he or she can. The remaining parent should be free to decide whether to take on a fulltime job without this kind of nonsensical prejudice.

Children of lone parents do less well at school – **false**. The children of lone parents often suffer an initial setback in their schooling as a result of the trauma of their situation. However, it does not need to last. Children of widows and widowers tend to do very well at school, recovering quickly from the distress. Children of broken marriages may need extra help because of the damage to self-esteem, but extra attention can reaffirm this and the children can succeed educationally.

You get more sympathy if your partner died – **true**. Families in which a parent died get more help and sympathy than families where a parent leaves. But the damage of the change is more in the families where there was breakdown. Such families need a great deal of encouragement and affirmation to re-establish life together.

Lone parents, especially women, are morally suspect – **false**. The morals of lone parents are much like the morals of the rest of the population. Many new lone parents find themselves shunned by friends of the family who don't know which of the couple to continue to include. Often the social circle has been related to the husband's life and work, and the lone mother finds herself with fewer friends just when she most needs them. Lone parents have a need for affirmation and encouragement that should not be confused with a sexual advance. Friendship is what she and the children need now.

It is harder for a male lone parent than a female – **false**. It is different. She may have more practice and training at childcare and housekeeping. He will almost undoubtedly have more money and more helping friends and relatives. He gets more sympathy if he is working and she gets more if she is not. The sympathy should be looked at in the light of the real circumstances each family is dealing with.

Children of lone parents are more likely to be delinquent – **false**. There is a high correlation between poverty and delinquency, and the rate of delinquency for children of lone parents is related to poverty, not to the fact that there is only one parent.

Self-image for the lone parent
Marriage breakdown, or the death of a partner, knocks at parents' sense of self-acceptance and ability to cope. A parent may crave some assurance about herself, as well as help in looking at the problems she now faces. For the sake of the whole family she should take time to talk to a professional counsellor, and if there is a family counsellor who can talk with the children too, that's ideal. As a parent and as a family they should have time to re-establish self-worth.

There are self-help groups for lone parents in most parts of the country. Many are extremely helpful with suggestions and mutual help. Some people have found them difficult as each group is as strong as its members and some may even be prone to gossip. Make sure that the ground rules of confidentiality and trust are being kept. Remember that most of the group are feeling vulnerable emotionally.[2]

Friends of lone parent families
Many times friends of single parents wonder how they can best help the family.

Never take over. However, find out if you can help.

Can you babysit sometimes?

Can you invite the whole family over for the day?

Can you take the children with you on an outing or on holiday?

Can you give a Christmas or birthday present?

Do you have smart clothes your children have grown out of which you can pass on, especially items of school uniform?

Can you invite the parent to adult social occasions at your house where she can re-establish friendships and make new ones?

Do you know of grants or benefits that the family could apply for to help them financially? Tell them.

Most children of lone parents lack a significant male adult in the family. By inviting them to be with your family you will be offering them some access to male company, games and friendships.

GRIEF

Whenever a major change happens in family life, members go through grief processes. To move house means the end of one set of relationships and the beginning of another. Small children will grieve for places and the order of life. Often a child of under-five dislikes even having her bed moved to a different part of the room. When planning to move house, explain what is happening and let her help with the packing so she sees where all the household pieces are boxed. Then she will know that what she fears lost is inside the boxes which are coming with them. Be especially careful that she is reassured about treasured toys and belongings. Be tolerant of any fears for them.

On arrival in the new home, help the child gradually become accustomed to a different playgroup, unfamiliar shops and people. Try to establish as much as possible of the child's routine just as it was before you moved. Try to avoid moving simultaneously with another major change in her life, for example when she is trying to cope with starting school.

A separation or divorce between parents is in many ways more difficult for a child to deal with than death. In addition to the loss, the remaining family members have feelings of rejection and guilt that are not easily resolved. The process of death and burial includes a long-established pattern or ritual that facilitates the necessary grieving time. There is no such process for family breakdown that externalises and facilitates the resolving of hurt feelings and disturbed lives. In addition, there is often anger and recrimination between the parents. Emotional security is violated for a child, with much less awareness of the effect of such events on children. Be as tolerant with a child's reactions to marriage breakdown and divorce as to death.

Footnotes
[1] *The Needs of Children* Mia Kellmer Pringle, Hutchinson.
[2] Your local library has a list of all groups meeting in your area, with details of whom to contact.

21. EXPECTATIONS AND PROBLEMS

Preparation for parenthood
Parents' decision to have children should be preceded by considerable conversation and resolution. Both should be prepared for compromising personal interests and ambitions. The responsibility for parenting cannot be effectively carried by one. Both parents should recognise the self-sacrifice that is demanded, the extra expense, the lost sleep, sickness, endless laundry, constant attention; and once begun, there is no turning back. The parents should have a great deal of mutual understanding and give-and-take in their own relationship so as to help one another with the changing identity and pressure that comes with a new baby.

Career satisfaction is often important to both women and men. Decide how you as a couple are going to cope with this when you have children. It is unreasonable to assume that one person will make all the sacrifices. A variety of careers now are making maternity leave available to women. It may be worth considering having children in your thirties when the career is established. Others within the company, recognising your skills, may then be more tolerant of temporary absence. For a man it is important to consider the changes to the amount of work that will need to be done at home. The extra work can be shared by both parents. Some couples find opportunity for job-sharing so that both may take equal care in child-rearing. For some, the man becomes the house-husband.

Whichever way a married couple sorts out these questions, they will find that the issues present themselves as pressures very quickly once there are children. It is easier to have talked at length beforehand and to have regular conversation as time passes than to wait till one or both are under considerable stress. For parents who are feeling the stress of unresolved pressures in family life there are many groups such as Marriage Encounter that give a safe environment for conversation at length.

Problems with children

All families have problems. To expect that a couple can get married and live happily ever after, like a fairy tale, only adds to the problems. A family can be strengthened by facing problems together and coming to terms with the family's internal stresses and conflicts. Myths about marriage and children are contributing factors in the cycle of disappointment and disillusion many young adults find in the reality of marriage and child rearing.

EXPECTATIONS

Expectations of one's spouse and of children begin in childhood and are built on in conversations, magazines, books, television and films. All of these sources tend toward an idealised image of the child, especially of babies. The same sources give idealised pictures of the kind of relationship father and mother have with one another.

When such expectations are denied by everyday experience the people involved will normally assume there is something wrong with themselves and their family; they may feel angry, guilty and depressed. It is difficult for those involved to realise that the *expectation* may be at fault. As a result, when expectations are not met and the conflict between the reality of

Expectations and Problems

everyday life and the high expectation goes unresolved, the family begins to suffer; the members may be causing and maintaining their own pressure.

A common expectation perpetrated by myth and media is that men will be earning a wage in a good job with excellent prospects for promotion. If (as is likely) they have no job and are unable to find one, their identity is under question, 'he is not a real man'. Unemployment has pushed millions of men into this questionable position – according to the myth. Where families are unable to look at the expectation and realise that it is based on unreality, the man becomes self-rejecting, despairing and sees fault in himself and his family. What he and his family need is a place to talk and come to terms with the gap between their expectations and the reality of the unemployment levels.

Pictures of mothers and babies, photographs, paintings, magazine stories and literature, depict peace and gentleness, a relaxed baby, smiling or sleeping, with a quiet and serene mother. Most babies are not like that, nor are most mothers. Babies cry, scream, demand, dirty themselves, create endless work and never say thank you. New mothers are tired, often discouraged, and are emotionally very vulnerable. Conversation between mothers can alleviate the pressure they may feel of not being a good mother because they don't measure up to the fairy tale mother of the romantic myth. Over a cup of tea, neighbours reminisce about how their baby was just as fretful, eventually grew out of it; how they never got the house tidy till the kids started school; how the only peace and serenity they ever got was when . . . The conversation abandons the high and unreal expectations for the more down to earth facts of everyday life with babies.

Parents do want to constantly love and affirm the child, never to give up on a crying baby, never fail to meet his needs. Recognising that no one is perfect, a mother who can abandon the expectation will go and relax a little, sit down in another room with a cup of tea for a few minutes. She knows that the baby is alright, changed, fed, and that sometimes babies cry themselves to sleep.

An isolated mother, who has high expectations and no friends and neighbours to talk to, may continue to be trapped by that expectation. She may become severely depressed at her own 'failure' with her child and consequently neglect them. She may become angry, interpreting crying as a message that she is failing or that the baby does not love her. She desperately wants his or her love, not realising the nature of a baby's love in being dependent, and it is in such circumstances that the mother can lose control and batter her baby.

Abuse
The stress of failed expectations, of living in very limited housing, tiny rooms with no space from the baby's crying can result in disorder, neglect and violence. Parents who sense that they may become violent in their frustration should ask for help. Ask the Health Visitor or Social Worker. Most helpful for you as parents will be the chance to talk over your pressures and air your expectations and disappointments. Some of the problems that have beset you and helped build the tension may be dispelled, and you may gain new insight into how to tackle the next problem.

Your near relatives, friends and neighbours will find it almost impossible to believe that you are near to hurting your baby, unless they grew up in a violent family. They may well simply try to pacify and reassure you that many people feel like that and never go beyond the feeling. However a remarkable number do. Many of those who abuse their children are ordinary people with impossible expectations of themselves and their family. Seek help from those who will take you seriously – before you are overcome by the pressure. Help can be given in the form of daycare facilities or nursery that will relieve the pressured situation and enable parents to find a more realistic perspective on life with children.

22. THE GIFT OF THE FAMILY

In the epistle to the Ephesians, Paul refers to the family in a number of ways. After talking about salvation and the future hope of glory, about the breaking down of barriers and hostility between people, Paul likens the family to the Trinity as he says: 'For this reason I bow my knees before the Father, from whom every family in heaven and on earth is named, that according to the riches of his glory he may grant you to be strengthened with might through his Spirit in the inner man, and that Christ may dwell in your hearts through faith; that you being rooted and grounded in love, may have power to comprehend with all the saints what is the breadth and length and height and depth, and to know the love of Christ which surpasses knowledge, that you may be filled with all the fulness of God.'

It is a remarkable revelation that the family is named after the fellowship in heaven.

In our families the nature of God may be revealed as we discover the qualities of friendship, acceptance, hope, encouragement, loyalty, forgiveness, gentleness and compassion. In the safe committed relationship of a family, of marriage, such qualities may be nurtured and matured. Marriage, where there is mutual givenness and friendship, has that special creativity of expression in bringing forth and nurturing children. What better environment for their growth could there be than a family in which the focus is the fellowship in heaven.

Such a vision for family life is not far-fetched even in the pressures of our society today once the starting point of the above passage is noted. Paul includes this passage to explain what he is praying for; he sees the potential of family life and prays for this for the people to whom he wrote. He was writing to a church and referring to a family in heaven, nevertheless we get from this a sense of direction for our prayers, for our families as well as our churches. We should pray for the rooting and grounding of love among us.

Gift of life

The gift of a child is a gift of life, and there is no breath of life without God, who himself has a special concern for children.

Throughout all of creation we see the regenerating and healing presence of life from God. Wounds heal and are forgotten. Trees and flowers, plants of all kinds, have within them such a force for life that they recover from uprooting, damage and disaster. Within a life-affirming environment the problems our children suffer, even those caused by our inadequate parenting, will on the whole heal and be forgotten. We can pray for and know that healing and regenerating grace for our children.

The positive attitudes made possible by our faith also help in times of adversity or stress. Remember this is God's world and through the Spirit he is always present to bring life.

Children and faith

Children have a vulnerable and precious faith in God, that is a gift to them and their parents.

King David, the prophet and priest Samuel, and Jesus all had faith in God while still children. The boy with the loaves and fishes showed his love for Jesus in a practical way. Such stories and the prayers and testimonies of our children can encourage us, and throw new light on adult views and attitudes. Parents often tell me stories of how their children have prayed, or have been very sure of what God was saying to the family and subsequent events have shown how close they were to him.

Sometimes the actions or attitudes of children may seem disturbing to parents, particularly as children grow older. Reflect on the story of Elisha abandoning his father to follow the prophet Elijah; Jonathan deceived his father King Saul to help David escape; and Jesus stayed behind in Jerusalem. We have record of Mary's response, but the parents in each situation were at least surprised and probably shocked. Yet God was calling and speaking to their children. The seeming disloyalty was seen later to be faithfulness to God.

Psalm 127 is a brief reflection on the house and the family with children. The family home is centred on the Lord, children are a gift from God. Happy is the family with 'a quiver full of them'. Children bring with them joy and laughter, fun and celebration. Both our friendship with our children and our family life are fulfilling and life-giving. Childhood includes many happy moments, a sense of freedom and enjoyment that is worth an immeasurable amount, and, as time spent with God, reflects to us the joys of the Kingdom.

APPENDIX

Growth and development patterns from 0–5 years old

physical development	*relationship development*
0 – 1	
rapid growth in weight and height.	from the security of relationship with mother, enjoys and is secure with other family members.
lifts head, rolls over, sits up without help, crawls, stands and begins to walk.	copes with other adults, such as babysitters, relatives
sleeps less each day but increasingly through the night.	If the child is clingy don't force them into new relationships, go slowly.

parents can:
affirm and encourage the child's exploration and curiosity,

provide colourful, safe toys of many textures, shapes, sizes and weights.

Offer new tastes, food and drinks,

put the baby where there's lots to see and touch.

Don't leave the baby lying with nothing to do or see.

Try not to compete with other parents about a child's natural development, each child has her own rate.

Appendix

1 – 2½ years old
crawls, walks, runs, though falls often, enjoys mother and toddler group climbs,

grows taller but not much heavier (reaches half adult height)

builds with simple blocks, looks at pictures, recognises some shapes

enjoys sand, water, noise makers,

rides a toddler bike, without pedals,

enjoys mother and toddler group,

becomes accustomed to other adult supervision,

has temper tantrums.

parents can:
expect the child to help put toys in toybox after playing,

expect her to begin feeding herself,

include outings to seaside, park, zoo, swimming pool, library, shops,

offer contact and play with other children, older as well as peers,

avoid using television to keep the child occupied. Watch only a few minutes each day.

Talk with them and tell stories.

Be sure to establish clearly the meaning of 'No' and other simple instructions.

3 – 4 years old
growth is less,

hops and skips, begins to catch ball, paints and colours, pedals a bike or car, climbs on climbing apparatus, plays in Wendy house and other role play,

joins playgroup and has significant contact with various adults and children,

begins to negotiate with other children in play.

parents can:
provide new experience and new people, include stories and books, and visits to the library, visit the zoo and the Science Museum, explore the countryside, seaside, town travel by train, bus, car.